AND ALL THAT

JENNIFER HARRIS, SARAH HYDE & GREG SMITH

DESIGN AND THE CONSUMER IN BRITAIN 1960-1969

TREFOIL
DESIGN
LIBRARY

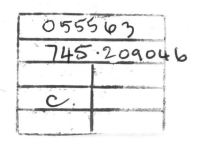
Published by
Trefoil Books Ltd.,
7 Royal Parade,
Dawes Road,
London SW6

Copyright © Whitworth Art Gallery

First published 1986

Set in Futura Light by Suripace Ltd., Milton Keynes,
and printed by R.J. Acford, Chichester.

Harris, Jennifer, 1949–
    1966 and all that! — (Trefoil design library)
    1. Design — Great Britain — History — 20th century
    I. Title II. Hyde, Sarah III. Smith, Greg
745.4'4941   NK928

ISBN 0-86294-087-7

The exhibition organisers would like to thank the following for
permission to reproduce photographs:

ABC Television, 90, 92; Airviews, Manchester Ltd., 63, 64, 65; BBC
Hulton Picture Library, 26; British Telecom Showcase, 129; Tom Brown,
81; Conran Octopus, I (photo by Clive Corless, from the Conran
Directory of Design, 1985); Continental Films, 5, 88; The Design
Council Picture Library and Archive, 19, 38, 39, 44, 45, 46, 47, 48, 115,
116, 121, XVI; Dodo Designs Ltd., 108, 113; EMI, 8, 107; James Galt
and Company Ltd., 31, 32, 33, 34; Gordon Russell Ltd., 44; Kenneth
Grange, 16; Henry Grant, 7; Greater London Council, 66, 67, 68, 69,
70, 75; Grosvenor Studios, Oxford, 127, 128; Hille International Ltd.,
42; Hoover Ltd., 123; Jaguar Cars, XV; London Regional Transport, III;
MGM, 101, 102 (courtesy of the National Film Archive Stills Library);
City of Manchester Art Galleries, XII; Manchester City Planning
Department, 77, 80; David Mellor, 56, 57; National Postal Museum,
19, 130, XVI; Private Eye, 6, 104; Race Furniture, 47; Rank Film
Distribution, 103 (courtesy of the National Film Archive Stills Library);
Adel Rootstein Display Mannequins Ltd., 85, 87; Professor Edgar Rose,
76; J Sainsbury plc, 23, 24, 25; Vidal Sassoon Salons, 95, 96; Michael
Seifert and Partners, XVIII; The Sunday Times Fashion Archive, Bath
Museum of Costume, 22; The Sunday Times Magazine, 9; Madame
Tussauds Ltd., 97; United Artists, 1; Vogue Magazine, 13, 21, 87, 98,
100 (reproduced by kind permission of Vogue. ©Conde Nast
Publications Ltd. Photographers: Peter Rand, Norman Parkinson, Cecil
Beaton, 'Just Jaeckin'); The Trustees of the Victoria and Albert
Museum, 50, 93, XIV; Warrington and Runcorn Development
Corporation, 35, 36, 41, 71, 82; Webb Corbett and Queensberry Hunt,
51, 53; Wolff Olins Ltd.

All other photographs by Peter Burton and Michael Pollard for the
Whitworth Art Gallery.

PITTV▯ ▯RNING
CENT ▯

UNIVERSITY OF
GLOUCESTERSHIRE
at Cheltenham and Gloucester

1966 and all that...

1966

CONTENTS

FOREWORD

Twenty years ago the Whitworth Art Gallery was bringing to completion the modernisation programme that has made it one of the most attractive and well appointed galleries in the country and there could be no more suitable location for an exhibition of design in the Sixties than here. Indeed, the gallery itself is a worthy exhibit in its own right. It is also appropriate that the exhibition should be looking at industrial design as we near our own centenary, for, when it was founded in 1889, the Whitworth Gallery had as one of its main objectives the encouragement of the links between design and industry in the north west. Sir Joseph Whitworth would, I am sure, have been delighted by the prospect of an exhibition dedicated to the design of mass-produced goods as the culmination of Manchester's contribution to Industry Year.

I would like to thank my staff for all their hard work on this exhibition. For a gallery the size of the Whitworth to take on such a prestigious and important project as this, at a time when cuts in our budget have meant cuts in our staff, requires an enormous amount of commitment and hard work. The exhibition has been selected and the catalogue written by Dr Jennifer Harris, Assistant Keeper of Textiles, Sarah Hyde, Assistant Keeper of Prints and Greg Smith, Research Assistant, Watercolours. I am also very grateful to Dr Nigel Whiteley, Head of the Department of Visual Arts, Lancaster University, for his thoughtful contribution.

To all lenders who are listed and acknowledged fully elsewhere in the catalogue, we extend our thanks, and also to those many people who have given so freely of their valuable time to discuss ideas with the staff of the Gallery. I am delighted to acknowledge the financial support of Virgin Retail Ltd and Marks & Spencer plc who have chosen once again to reaffirm their commitment to arts sponsorship.

Professor C. R. Dodwell
Director

ACKNOWLEDGEMENTS

We would particularly like to thank our colleagues at the Whitworth Art Gallery for all their help in the preparation of the exhibition, and of this catalogue, and in particular Joanna Banham, Lynda Black, Cliff Lomax, Laura Milligan, Susan Mortimer, Julian Tomlin, John West, Sara Williams and Eve Winson. Our thanks also to the following people for helping in a variety of ways: Airviews, Manchester; Elizabeth Anson; Penelope Byrde of Bath Museum of Costume; Irene Bayliss; Jonathan Bennett; Robert Pirie and Janet Hyde of BOC; Ron Whitehead of the British Motor Industry Heritage Trust; Andrew and Susan Causey; Beverly Cowburn; Pam Beavill and Fiona McDonald of the Design Council; Bridget Kinally and Judith Powling of the Design Council Photograph Library; Robin Farrow and Paula McGibbon of Dodo Designs Ltd; Eliot Nixon of the John Doran Gas Museum; Alastair Forsyth; Mrs Vere French; James Offer of James Galt and Company Ltd; Mrs Rosemary Ransome-Wallis at Goldsmith's Hall; Ray Leigh of Gordon Russell Ltd; Kenneth Grange; Gwyneth Marshall of the Department of Town Planning and Architecture, Greater London Council; Liz Hall, Cherrill Scheer of Hille Ltd; George Harrison, Director of the History of Advertising Trust; Mr T Roylance of ICI Ltd Design Department (Wallcoverings); Ian Luckett of Special Facilities, Jaguar Cars Ltd.; Delia Watkins of KMP Partnership; Wendy Evans of the Museum of London; Jonathan Riddell of London Transport Museum and Peter Durrant of London Regional Transport; Ian Logan; Veronica Tonge of Maidstone Museum and Art Gallery; the staff of Manchester Central Reference Library, in particular the Local History Library; Maurice Davies of Manchester City Art Gallery; Roy Mitchell of the Model Making Department, Manchester City Planning Department; Anne Miller of Manchester Polytechnic Library; Professor Roger Stonehouse and Roderick Males of Manchester University School of Architecture; Ross Herzog of Manchester Urban Studies Centre; David Mellor; Alex Moulton; Susan Bennett of the National Book League; John Memmott of the National Postal Museum, London; Wally Olins; Mary Alexander of Pentagram Design Ltd; Eddie Pond; Penny Thompson of Portsmouth City Art Gallery; Louise Barnett at Mary Quant Ltd; Lord David Queensberry; Les Smith of Race Furniture Ltd; Catherine Rew; Professor Edgar Rose; Bridget Williams, Archivist of J. Sainsbury plc; Christine Woods, Archivist at

Arthur Sanderson and Sons Ltd; Joanne Rix of Vidal Sassoon's; Katie Scott; Richard Seifert and Joyce Chidlow of R. Seifert and Partners; Graham Whitehead of Skelmersdale New Town Commission; Gill Hedley of Southampton City Art Gallery; Neil Johannessen of Telecom Technology Showcase; Catherine Upton; Stephen Astley, Clive Wainwright, Margaret Timmers and Charles Newton of the Victoria and Albert Museum; Cathy Cripwell of the Victoria and Albert Museum Archive of Art and Design; Mark Nicholls and Emma Ward of Virgin Retail; Elaine Shaw of *Vogue* magazine; Nigel Walters; Harry Ward; Mr Canning of Warrington Runcorn Development Corporation; Robert Welch; Bridget Moorman, Librarian at Wolff Olins Ltd.; Ian Wolfenden; Greg Stevens of Wrighton International; Hilary McGowan and Mark Suggitt at York Castle Museum.

Our warmest thanks also go to all the visitors to the Whitworth Art Gallery who so freely offered their Sixties items for our exhibition, and to our Director, Professor C. R. Dodwell, and Principal Keeper, Francis Hawcroft, for their continued support throughout the project. Thanks also to Melissa Denny of Trefoil Books.

Jennifer Harris
Sarah Hyde
Gregory Smith

Exhibition designed by Alasdair Hamilton
Additional research by Denise Seneviratne
Photography by Peter Burton and Michael Pollard
Sponsored by Virgin Retail and Marks & Spencer plc

INTRODUCTION

"Sexual intercourse began in nineteen sixty-three
(Which was rather late for me) –
Between the end of the *Chatterley* ban
And the Beatles' first L.P."

From *Annus Mirabilis* by Philip Larkin

STUDYING THE SIXTIES

The study of history by decades (decadeism) is very much a twentieth-century idea, and stems from the historically questionable belief that life now is changing faster than ever before. Retrospectively parcelling off one decade from another is, as Nigel Whiteley demonstrates below, a gross oversimplification of the complex, contradictory nature of history. But, decadeism is not entirely invalid as an historical tool since it works in the other direction too, in the sense that each decade ended and celebrated brings in a new decade of hopes. Thus *Queen* magazine produced a special 'BOOM' issue in 1959 which announced that 'Britain has launched into an age of unparalleled lavish living'. 'FACING THE CRAZY SIXTIES' the headlines announced; 'THE TENSE PRESENT!' Harold Wilson in 1960 announced a similar agenda for the Sixties in a speech at Scarborough. 'This is our message for the Sixties. A socialist scientific and technological revolution releasing energy on an enormous scale'.[1] The contributors to the 'What's wrong with Britain?' debate and the proponents of 'You've never had it so good' were united by the belief that the turning decade stood for something, whether a source of self-congratulation or the start of an exciting future.

Ten years later, and on the threshold of another new decade, Britain was demonstrably better off, and had changed culturally and socially more than would have seemed possible in 1960. Opinions, however, were still divided; people were not a little bewildered by the pace of the self-willed charge into the future. In the journalistic clichés of the day, the Sixties were summed up as a series of polarities: exciting/hysterical, idealistic/cynical, affluent/soulless, liberated/corrupt. As the Sixties drew to a close, a consensus view about society was as far away as ever.

Nearly twenty years on, views of the decade are just as entrenched, just as polarised. An amusing update of *1066 And All That* could be written to deflate the misconceptions and over-simplifications which we cherish when considering the Sixties, just as much as the schoolchild's version of history is gently mocked in the earlier work.[2] There is, however, a serious side to this. Over the past year or two 'the Sixties' have entered the contemporary political arena. The decade has been

9

held up as a warning: as an age of moral decline, an example of overweening state bureaucracy; others have offered it as an example of idealism, optimism and energy that could enrich our own cynical age[3]. A decade which can be used to support such polarised views must be worth investigating. If the desperate search for an identity in the Sixties stemmed from uncertainty (Britain, in the words of Dean Acheson 'had lost an empire and not yet found a role'),[4] then our own evident obsession with the Sixties reflects a new age of uncertainty: we have lost our industrial base and found no alternative.

DESIGN AND THE SIXTIES

Design plays a significant part in everybody's conception of the Sixties. Asked to sum up the decade briefly, people invariably focus on one or two objects designed during the Sixties: mini-skirt, mini-car or the cover of a Beatles LP as though they have the symbolic power to encapsulate an era. Fine art and crafts, as well as design and architecture produced for a rich clientele are certainly 'of the period' but the terms in which they are normally discussed, namely the artist/designer/patron nexus seem to exclude them from many people's image of the Sixties. When all but the youngest readers will have had first hand experience of the period, it would be missing a golden opportunity not to concentrate on those objects which are closest to people's interests.

Studies of design in the period 1960-1969 have, on the whole, so far failed to add much of substance to our understanding of the decade. In spite of the challenge of the Pop style, the term 'design' is still equated with 'good design' in many circles. Museums and writers who consider their primary function as guiding public taste, have presented the history of design as a series of Design Council award-winning objects which would have been found in only a tiny minority of houses in the Sixties. At the same time the opposite approach, of presenting objects which conform to popular notions of Sixties style (that is, fashion, graphics, furniture, etc, which are brash, colourful, steamlined or modern) in an uncritical way, has done little more than confirm a simplified view of history and further fuelled the Sixties nostalgia boom.

It seems then, that what is needed to understand a decade is a rather more inclusive, popular definition of design, which can encompass everything we wear, the objects we use, and the buildings we live and work in. If you had entered any room, in any house, during the Sixties, it would have contained a large number of items that were not designed in that decade. Even those goods which had been bought during the Sixties were more than likely to have been very conservative in appearance. Therefore the picture put forward, both by those who analyse only what they consider to be 'good' design, and by those who only study innovative designs of the period, is necessarily a very limited one.

This said, however, we still believe that it is defensible to consider a group of goods introduced during the decade as there is no-one who could not have been touched by, or at least aware of, some of the items discussed. Whilst accepting that a truly populist approach would include more items from the pages of a Littlewoods catalogue than those designed by Mary Quant or to be found at Habitat, we would argue that it is not these truly 'popular' goods that people pick out to symbolise the period. It is not a diffuse definition of design that is needed then but a more analytical approach which can put the familiar in a new light.

Central to this approach is the belief that design is not a vague reflection of the mood of the period, or the triumphant problem-solving product of a designer of genius. Design can transform ideas about who we are, how we should behave, and the standards to which we should conform, into physical forms. Design does not simply provide images of shared ideas, beliefs or needs, it also has an active role: it can change our behaviour and confirm, or call into question, our prejudices. This must be considered in any analysis of the period. Taken at their face value, designed goods promote little more than the sort of definition that equates the Sixties with mini-skirts, and mini-skirts with freedom. By looking at design as an active process we can begin to analyse the development and maintenance of the many myths which surround the Sixties. As Adrian Forty has suggested, it is the capacity of design to embody and 'to cast myths into an enduring, solid and tangible form, so that it seems to be reality itself'[5] which is the attraction of design for those who wish to probe beneath the surface.

Given the nature of what at times seems to be an obsessional interest in the Sixties, the sort of design history proposed here is not just an attempt at putting the historical record straight but something that might take its place in a rather broader debate. By looking at the Sixties, both at the myths propagated then, and the myths current today, as well as the complex, contradictory reality of the period, it is possible to understand more about contemporary society as well as allowing us to make a more informed leap into the future.

DESIGNING THE CONSUMER

The post-war period has frequently been described as having given birth to the consumer society, and yet surprisingly few discussions of design have considered the consumer in any detail. Whether presented as the uncritical praise of the latest fad or fashion or as part of the consumer boom statistic, the consumer's role has been consistently marginalised. Given the nature of human curiosity it is surprising that questions such as how much something cost, where it could be bought and what it meant to own a particular item are usually excluded from discussions on design. Consumers are frequently mentioned in general terms but their individual voices, compared to that of, say, the designer, are conspicuous by their silence.

Compared with its absence in recent discussions on design, the debate during the Sixties about consumer interests was widespread and was conducted against the background of a growing awareness of the sophistication of marketing and advertising techniques. A particularly important debate was sparked off by the artist Richard Hamilton who, in a lecture to the I.C.A. (reprinted in *Design*, February 1960), defended the notion, widely accepted in America, of planned obsolescence, and argued that since it increased production it was a 'basic social good'. More controversially Hamilton suggested that, if designers wished to produce popular designs, they must follow the American pattern and work closely with market and 'motivation' researchers and with advertisers so as to 'design a consumer to the product'. This last point was particularly difficult for *Design* magazine to accept. In an editorial titled 'Consumers in Danger' it was suggested that Hamilton's view that 'the consumer can come from the same drawing board (as the product)' was a form of 'economic totalitarianism'. The debate that followed saw a split between the conservative cultural critics besotted by the threat of Americanisation, and those who saw Hamilton's vision of the future as an inevitable consequence of the 'consumer boom'.

Studies of the media were a Sixties' growth industry and readers of Vance Packard's *The Hidden Persuaders* or Marshall McLuhan's analysis of the power of the media were in the forefront of the reaction against the rampant materialism that set in later in the decade. But in 1960 a surprisingly large number of people did not have a fridge or a telephone, and in the ensuing decade the electrical appliance companies, and all the rest, had a field day.

A less spectacular, but rather more significant, reaction to unbridled consumerism than the 'drop out' ethic, was the rise of the Consumer Movement. Compared with America the movement was slow to develop, but in 1957 a new group, the Association for Consumer Research Ltd (later the Consumers' Association), was founded and published the first issue of *Which?* magazine. The concept of comparative testing, objective standards of performance, and value for money were a real breakthrough. By 1967 *Which?* had 434,000 subscribers. Together with the introduction of the British Standards 'Kite' mark, and in the same year the passing of the Trades Description Act, the magazine helped to safeguard the consumer position.

The consumers' role in capitalism, whatever design historians may argue, is to consume, and the primary role of the designer is to produce the goods which are to be consumed. A successful, that is to say profitable, product is not necessarily one which fulfils deeply felt needs – take the paper dress, for instance – or one which creates an enriching aesthetic experience. Rather, the product is shaped by a design which can 'incorporate the idea that will make it marketable'.[6] If we are to understand how design works and, indeed, shapes the fabric of a capitalist society we need, as the media commentators of the period insisted, to look at design in the context of advertising, marketing and retailing. Only then can we understand the real role of design: to sell goods.

Notes

1. Francis Wheen, *The Sixties*, London, 1984, p 54
2. W B Sellar and R J Yeatman, *1066 And All That*, London, 1930
3. See David Edgar, 'It wasn't so naff in the '60s after all', *The Guardian*, July 7, 1986
4. See Bernard Levin, *The Pendulum Years, Britain in the Sixties*, London 1967, p 236
5. Adrian Forty, *Objects of Desire: Design and Society 1750-1980*, London 1986, p 9
6. Ibid, p 9

SHAPING THE SIXTIES

Nigel Whiteley

Whether you remember it with affection or loathing, think of it as a time of unbridled creativity or of moral decay, you will probably admit that the 1960s seemed to have a mood and character that was distinctive and very different from any time before or since. That mood and character is reflected in the objects and images of the time. Why is it that the mini car and an Op art mini dress, a David Bailey photograph, some disposable paper furniture and a transistor radio epitomise what is popularly-termed the 'swinging Sixties'? Just what was it that *shaped* the design we so readily identify with that decade?

The Sixties have been mythologised more than most decades. The epithet 'swinging' is a journalistic invention, the result of the feature-writer's alarming appetite for alliteration, cliche, and sensationalism. Selective memory, wishful thinking and instant nostalgia have also contributed to our current caricatured view. Now is the time to stop both the uncritical nostalgic celebrations *and* the point-scoring political castigations of the 'permissive Sixties' so that we can begin to analyse the decade dispassionately. The first thing we need to do is to pluck the decade out of the over-simplification that results from the current *penchant* for pigeon-holing and categorising 20th century history by decades. This will help us to see the 1960s as part of an historical process and as a series of post-war developments and trends. It will enable us to understand the forces that were *shaping the Sixties*.

There were three distinct phases to the 1960s and two of them overlapped with the adjoining decades. The first phase, which ends around 1962, can be traced directly back to the mid-1950s; the second — the one which tends to attract the epithet 'swinging' — lasted between roughly 1962 and 1967 (and so constituted only about half the decade); the third phase occurs between about 1967/8 and the early to mid-1970s. The final phase marks a change of sensibility, especially pronounced amongst the young.

It was the effects of earlier change — a change of economic conditions and of social attitudes — that formed the basis of the 'first phase' of the Sixties. The common mood of social idealism which flourished in the later years of the Second World War had, in the 1945 election, resulted in a landslide victory for the Labour party with its commitment to a comprehensive welfare state. Labour's term of office was, to a large extent inevitably, an austere time: resources were scarce,

1 The Mini Minor, as featured in *The Knack*, a 1965 film directed by Richard Lester.

2 Ronson's dryer, the 'Rio', designed by Kenneth Grange and first produced in 1966, weighed only 4oz more than the Braun dryer (fig. 2), and sold for £4 19s 6d in 1967.

3 The small, lightweight Braun hairdryer is an example of the kind of 'good design' promoted by Terence Conran through his Habitat stores during the Sixties. The price of Braun's appliances was formidable; this hairdryer cost £8 10s in 1967, whilst a similar model by Morphy Richards cost £4 0s 9d.

4 Front covers of Design magazine for October and December, 1967. The logotype used for the magazine's title was designed by Kenneth Garland and was first used on the January 1962 issue.

money was tight and consumer goods were manufactured for export only. Basic foods and clothing were all strictly rationed until at least 1948 and, in many cases, until 1950 with the last controls terminated only in 1954. It was against this background of impatience and even disillusionment that the Conservatives, under the leadership of Winston Churchill, were returned to power in 1951 with an electioneering promise to 'Set the People Free'. After the selflessness and sacrifices of the war and the self-denying frugality of the post-war period, people wanted to reap material rewards and enjoy consumer pleasures. And so they did. During the 1950s private affluence substantially increased for the vast majority of the population, particularly during the latter half of the decade. Between 1955 and 1960 – a period of low inflation – the weekly wage rose by an average of 25 percent. When overtime is taken into account, weekly *earnings* shot up dramatically by 34 percent.[1] At a time of full employment this affected not only the middle-classes but also working-class families, many of whom now found they had for the first time some disposable income. Few could argue with Prime Minister Harold MacMillan's oft-quoted 1957 remark that 'You've never had it so good.' One example of the new affluence – and one which was to have major social and environmental consequences in the 1960s – was the sharp rise in car ownership which jumped by a massive 250 percent between 1951 and 1961.[2] Another indication was the multiplication of television sets: in 1951 only six percent of households had one but a decade later that number had risen to 75 percent.[3]

Changes were not only quantitative but qualitative. By 1959, 60 percent of British adults were tuning in to television for an average of five hours every evening in the winter and three and a half hours on a summer evening. And, to a ratio of 3:1, they were watching *commercial* television. The Independent Television Company (ITV), which had commenced broadcasting in 1955, professed to know what the public really wanted and presented programmes of a tone quite different from that of the Reithian-influenced BBC. Critics were worried by the effect of all this viewing. Was it reducing once interactive family groups to passive and isolated individuals? Perhaps even worse, was commercial television fuelling materialism through American programmes? and was advertising creating false desires for new, bigger and supposedly better consumer goods? Opinions about the qualitative effects may have varied but the underlying trend of increasing private affluence was undeniable. One effect on design was obvious — people had more money to spend on goods. Another was less immediately obvious but major in its implications — *social mobility*. The new wealth and a more meritocratic educational system altered opportunities and expectations. Young adults who would previously have been expected to retain the aspirations and roles of their parents were genuinely able to break with convention. By the mid-1950s only one man in three had the same social status (by occupation) as his father, and only one son in four of an unskilled labourer remained unskilled. Many young couples craved the social status of their own homes followed by the cars, cookers, refrigerators, washing machines, kettles, toasters, food mixers, televisions, radios and record players that constituted the

5 Criticising the narrowness of the range of the items which the CoID considered worthy of design awards during the Sixties, the designer Michael Wolff wrote in the Journal of the Society of Industrial Arts in 1965, that 'the sort of designers in Britain who have really given people a bang in the last two years are Ken Adams, Art Director of the James Bond films; Frederick Starke with his clothes for Cathy Gale; and Ray Cusick, with his daleks.'

material dreams that money could buy.

Social mobility radically altered the *role* of design. Stated simply, no longer was it mainly a question of *whether* you owned, say, a new radio, but *which make or type*. As the division between a 'have/have not' society was replaced by a society in which ownership became the norm, the role of design and the appearance of products underwent a gradual but significant shift. Design was beginning to be used as a social language. The make and model of a product could confer prestige and status on its owner. Your choice of goods, like the decoration of your house and your taste in clothes, helped to communicate how you saw your place in the world and position in society. That you possessed a hairdryer by Braun rather than one by Ronson began to *matter*. Product styling and advertising became the key means of giving a product a distinct identity and loading it with social meaning and status. As competition became fiercer so a positive identity became crucial to a product's success.

Looking back it is remarkable how little those who were supposed to be in touch with design realised what was happening, let alone its significance. The Council of Industrial Design (CoID), for example, seemed quite unable to come to terms with the changes in society and design. Born of the social idealism of the late war years, the CoID seemed to find it hard to shake off a tone which was memorably described by the critic Reyner Banham as '...all Montgomery and sodawater...',[4] continuing to talk in increasingly outdated jingoistic terms of (in the words of the editor of the CoID's magazine *Design*) the '...fight against the shoddy design of those goods by which most of our fellow-men are surrounded...'[5] The criteria of 'good design' as far as the CoID was concerned

PRIVATE EYE

No. 40
Friday
28 June 63

Price 1/-

Spare us, O Ward,
Thy Further Revelations
until just before an
October Election

6 Front cover of *Private Eye*, June 1963. The caption refers to Stephen Ward, who had introduced the Minister of War, John Profumo, to show-girl Christine Keeler, and was later convicted of living off immoral earnings. In the following October Labour did win the election, though by a narrow majority.

were established, fixed and non-negotiable. Any unwillingness by the public to embrace the kind of products the CoID approved therefore signified that the '...docile and uncritical public is not conducive to a high standard of design.'[6] People did not, in other words, know what was good for them, preferring instead '...vulgar and boastful design...'[7] Some critics suspected that the CoID was in reality little interested in good design which, in most definitions, is centrally concerned with efficient working order, but with 'good taste'. Indeed the CoID paid scant regard to ergonomic tests and even criticised the consumer magazines for paying *too much* attention to them.[8] With the naivety that often accompanies either ignorance or arrogance, a spokesman asserted in 1961 that the CoID's intention was

> '...less to provide a guide to what is best on the market than to suggest, through a close study of individual products, what are the things that really matter in design...'[9]

It was, in effect, little more than a certain *type* of taste – professional (or 'narrow'[10]) middle class taste – that the Council was upholding. The CoID's pronouncements reflected its taste – and class – preferences, and it was scathingly dubbed by Banham 'H.M. Fashion House'.[11] The conflicting outlooks of the CoID and certain critics in the 1950s and early 1960s are instructive because they were symptomatic of some of the major changes in British culture and society in that period. The main battlegrounds were values, attitudes, and taste. Each was reinforced and emphasised by the other two.

Changes in value are often misinterpreted by those who uphold an established code of values as a lowering of *standards* . This was certainly the case during the later 1950s and 1960s. A value system which had endured for twenty to thirty years was being rapidly and, for many, painfully superseded. In design we can see it in terms of the widening gulf between the CoID (with its essentially Modernist value system derived from the writings and teachings of men like *Bauhausler* Walter Gropius and Le Corbusier), and critics such as Reyner Banham who sought a more populist, socially-orientated view of design in keeping with the post-war age of the mass media and consumerism.[12] Those whose values had been derived from Modernism were appalled by the apparent 'lowering of standards'. Herbert Read, a leading British Modernist, bitterly complained that society had come to the situation wherein

> 'The supermarket and the bargain basement replace the museums and art galleries as repositories of taste, and any ideals of beauty or truth, refinement or restraint, are dismissed, in the language of the tribe, as "square".'[13]

Here we are witnessing one side of the kind of head-on collision that could be observed in virtually all walks of life at the time including television (the criticisms of commercialisation and depersonalised American mass media values); the family (the breakdown of traditional roles); society (increased lawlessness); sex and courtship; and the decline of religion.

As important as the *fact* of the conflict of values was the *tone* of disagreement. A profound shift was occurring in attitudes, at the heart of which was the attitude to authority and authorities. The tone is epitomised by the so-called 'Angry Young Men', a conglomeration of writers and critics who included John Osborne, Kenneth Tynan, John Wain, Lindsay Anderson and Colin Wilson. In design, some

7 Carnaby Street, photographed in 1968 by Henry Grant; Union Jack flags and a colourful mural above the 'Lord John' boutique fail to produce the air of excitement that 'the world' came to Carnaby Street to see.

younger critics were equally disrespectful towards what they saw as the design establishment. One criticised the latter for its '...position of moral self-righteousness (which is) no different from that of the sermonising total abstainer.'[14] The insurrection had begun and anti-establishmentarianism, as inelegantly named as it was impolitely mannered, had arrived. As a movement, anti-establishmentarianism reached its apotheosis with the satire boom of the early 1960s. 'That Was The Week That Was" and *Private Eye* lambasted and ridiculed politicians, high court judges and other guardians of the nation's values more cruelly than had anyone in living memory. As a mood, anti-establishmentarianism remained, throughout the decade, a tool exploited to great effect by the young in the ensuing battle of the generations.

Values and attitudes are manifested in a group's *taste*, the third of the historic battlefields we are currently visiting. Before post-war consumerism, an individual's taste in what we now call 'lifestyle' tended to echo the taste of his or her parents and was a reliable indicator of their social class. The affluence that created disposable income for the middle and more prosperous echelons of the working classes, and its corollary, social mobility, created both design's new role and a subsequent change in the structure of taste. Your taste proclaimed your hopes, aspirations and outlook: it now revealed not just who you were and where (in social terms) you had come from but, to the extent you could afford it,

8 Cover for the Beatles' *Revolver,*
Parlaphone 1966, with line drawings
and collage by Klaus Voorman.

9 *The Sunday Times Magazine,* 3
August, 1969, included the first pictures
taken by astronauts on the surface of
the moon.

how you *wanted to be seen* by the rest of society. In the age of consumerism the old idea of a singular 'good' or correct taste was being replaced by a social and plural view in which taste was an expression of a group's identity and outlook.

The new and significant group in the 1960s was youth. Youth became an identifiable market for two reasons. First and foremost was the economic factor; youth had disposable income in enticing quantities and so it became a much sought-after consumer target group as manufacturers attempted to fulfil youth's perceived needs and desires. Second was its demographic increase. The post-war 'baby boom' resulted in a large increase of 15 to 19 year-olds as a percentage of the total population. From the 1955 level of 6.5 percent this rose to just under eight percent in 1963 and 1964 – the highest level for over a century – before settling at around seven percent in the late 1960s and 1970s. The combination of these two factors along with changing social attitudes and values gave these '...children of the Age of Mass-Communication...'[15] an outlook which marked them out from the past and a confidence that to many was as outrageous as it was brash.

In 1959 *Vogue* had noted that 'young' was appearing '... as the persuasive adjective for all fashions, hairstyles, and ways of life.'[16] By 1963 the media had become almost obsessed with youth values, youth trends and youth idols. 1963 has been described as '...the year the 1950s ended':[17] it was the year that Britain seemed to explode into Pop. It was less than a decade between the abolition of all rationing and the rise of Beatlemania, but it seemed like a century. From the Beatles to Mary Quant and from Carnaby Street to Liverpool, Britain became the mecca of Pop. The Beatles' first LP, *Please Please Me,* was number one in the charts for six months and in the top ten for a total of 61 weeks. *With the Beatles* and *A Hard Day's Night,* both released in 1964, were in the top ten of the British LP charts for a total of 75 weeks. America reacted in the same way. At one time in 1964 the Beatles held the top five places in the American singles charts with 12 records in the top one hundred. Britain's position as the leader in Pop music was undisputed.

This was equally true in fashion. Fashion became a topic of national interest and debate in 1963 – the year when '...legs never had it so good.'[18] The mini had arrived although, at this stage it was long enough to be worn by women of all ages.

The person who, in the public's eyes, represented the new mood in fashion was Mary Quant who was presented as the fashion equivalent of the Beatles. Her trip to America in 1962 was highly successful and helped to establish British leadership in young fashions. A year later critics were claiming that she had changed the whole approach of the British to fashion. Quant herself was more modest about her achievement: 'We were in at the beginning of a tremendous renaissance in fashion. It was not happening because of us. It was simply that, as things turned out, we were part of it.'[19] Quant (and two partners) had actually opened her 'Bazaar' boutique in 1955 but it was the early 1960s before the market conditions were ripe for development. From then on the market grew as the designers blossomed.

Young fashion designers who achieved a rapid rise to fame in 1962 and 1963 included Zandra Rhodes, Bill Gibb, Ossie Clark, and Marion Foale and Sally Tuffin. Foale and Tuffin typified the new young designers. They left the Royal

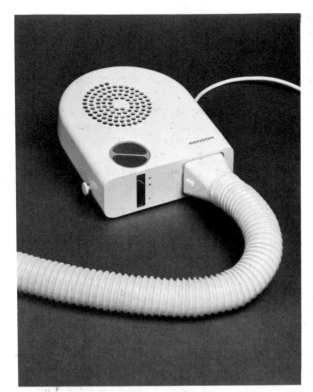

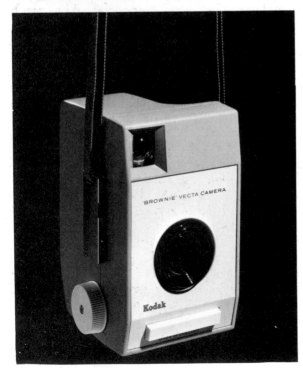

College of Art in 1961 and declared 'We...don't want to be chic; we just want to be ridiculous.'[20] They were not dictating a new fashion from above but were themselves a part of it — so much so that they were able to say that'...we only design clothes that we want to wear.'[21] The trade journal the *Tailor and Cutter* was forced to acknowledge that '...for the first time ever, many fashion influences are emanating from the under-25 group'.[22] 'Mod', used both as a noun and an adjective, became the blanket term for these young female and male styles. In 1964 the International Fashion Council officially acknowledged the youth market as a 'style of fashion'. Fashion may have been breaking down barriers of class and nationality but it was creating a new condition of membership: age.

It was in male fashions that the shock of the new was at its greatest. Up to the time of Pop, male clothes were sombre and discreet, a direct descendant of puritan dress and an expression of seriousness of mind. Any extrovert display was taken as a snub to decorum and good taste. If a woman's clothing was supposed to make her attractive to the opposite sex, the motivation behind men's fashion was, conventionally, to denote status. The suspicion that only homosexual men were interested in fashion — a characteristic of the puritan tradition — was another reason for the sense of outrage caused by Pop fashions and a major contributor to the ever-widening 'generation gap'. Unisex hairstyles and clothes caused an outcry from older generations brought up to expect gender differentiation. The *Tailor and Cutter* sternly cautioned: 'Adopting girls' hair styles may lead to adopting their clothes and there is legal danger in that.'[23] The same magazine was equally horrified by the visual outrageousness and poor physical quality of new clothing bemoaning the '...new concentration on visual impact at the *complete expense* of quality (in its old connotation of durability).' [24] But expendability — whether physical *or* stylistic — and the condition of continual change were the very essence of Pop.

Fashion had also become a form of non-verbal communication. In 1964 and 1965 a lot of Pop groups wore clothes far more outrageous and had their hair far longer than the mild-mannered and semi-respectable Beatles. The Rolling Stones and the Pretty Things were two groups who cultivated a scruffy appearance and acted rebelliously with public displays of bad manners. Bad press reports followed but, working under the premise that all press coverage is, *per se*, good, the groups were encouraged in their rowdyism.

Fashion and music were (and remain) the two interlocking matrices of youth culture. Graphic design played a supporting role but did not fully come into its own until hippy content and graphic form were fused in the psychedelic craze of 1967. What was typically Pop in the 1960s was the visual eclecticism that could be observed on everything from tea towels to record covers. The Beatles' LP covers alone reveal stylistic debts to a multitude of sources including Pop Art (the Warholian *Hard Day's Night* and the Peter Blake collaged *Sgt Pepper*); Art Nouveau (the Beardsley-inspired *Revolver*); psychedelia (the distorted *Rubber Soul*); Surrealism (*Abbey Road*); comic strip (*Yellow Submarine*); and the 1920s (the Gatsby-style *Collection of Beatles' Oldies*). Graphic designs were plundered from Op and Pop Art and indiscriminately applied to an indeterminable number of objects.

Product design featured little in Pop. In the vast majority of cases a product's Pop-ness resulted from the decoration applied to it, not from a redesign of its

10 The Ronson 'Courier'.

11 The 'Brownie' Vecta camera was designed by Kenneth Grange in 1966 for Kodak. Grange argued that the commonest type of photograph taken by amateurs was portrait format featuring two people, and that the landscape format field of vision usual in most cameras was not particularly well suited to the sort of market targeted by Kodak.

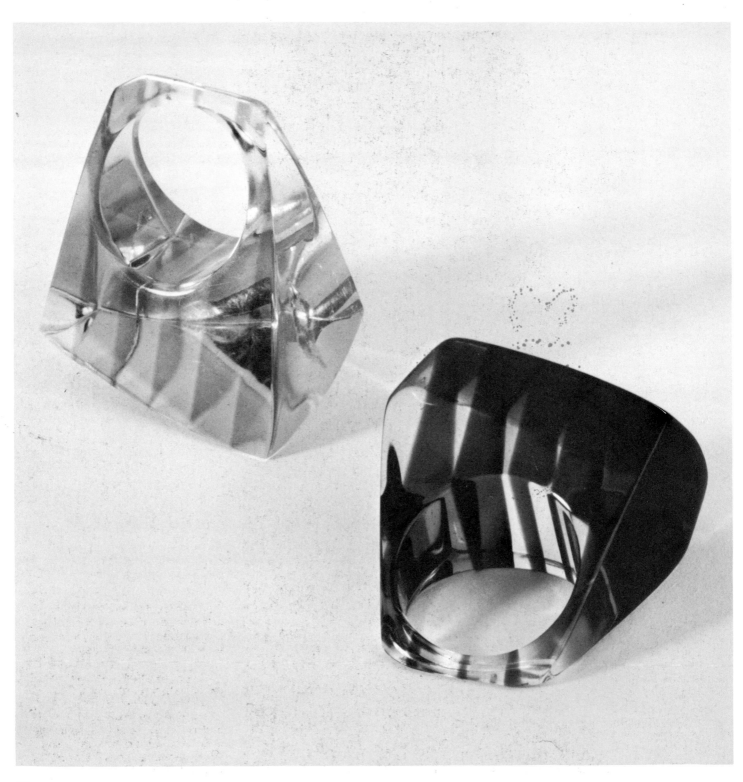

12 Brightly coloured futuristic imagery in the shape of perspex rings, so large and hard that they severely restricted the wearer's manual dexterity.

13 *Vogue* described this as a 'Snap crackle pop dress of sliver-fine silver, metal covered melinex which is virtually indestructible...sold in a pack and made in a second, this noisy little dress sells for 16s at Peter Robinson...' Photographed by Peter Rand for British *Vogue*, January 1967.

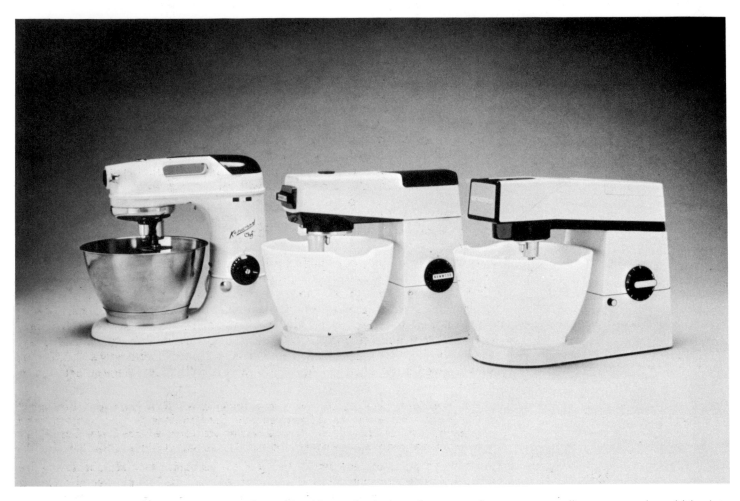

14 Kenneth Grange's 1961
modernisation of Kenwood's 'Chef'
mixer, shown here with, to the left, the
model in production until 1960, and, to
the right, the only slightly altered form
introduced when the mechanics were
updated in 1975.

form. The Union Jack mug, for example, was originally mass produced blank in tens of thousands, and any image ranging from different pop groups, through signs of the zodiac to football teams or vintage cars could be printed on it. Although the subject matter of the Beatles' mug was Pop, its form could have come out of the Bauhaus. Some furniture, on the other hand, was undeniably Pop. The Pop devotee, quite understandably, did not want to come home to a living room full of 'Scandinavian modern' or repro-antiques. Max Clendinning, a young furniture designer, had claimed that the mini would radically affect furniture design and, from the mid-1960s, he was proved right. It happened in two ways. The first was the application to furniture of the type of bold and decorative graphic patterns that were to be seen on mini skirts. The second was the transference of the *attitude* towards the mini – namely that furniture could be disposable, fashionable and fun. Paper furniture was all these things. Designed for maximum visual impact its lifespan was only a matter of months – but by then the colourful pattern may already have worn down the owner's tolerance. Or it may have just become out of fashion, the inevitable casualty of the age of disposability.

The essence of Pop, as a fashion journalist so accurately observed in 1965, was its '...enjoy-it-today-sling-it-tomorrow...' [25] mentality. Between 1963 and 1967 Carnaby Street, the fashion and commercial centre, became the focus of attention and popular symbol of 'swinging Britain' and the Pop style. The street's gaudy Pop Art colours and fun imagery gelled to such an extent that, in the words of Ken and Kate Baynes in a 1966 article in *Design* , 'One day "Carnaby Street" could rank with "Bauhaus" as a descriptive phrase for a design style...'[26] And yet Pop was so much more than a mere style or even series of impactful and expendable styles. It was nothing less than an attitude, a stance and an outlook on life. Pop was about being young and feeling young, about jettisoning the past and living in an ever-changing present with an eye to an exciting and challenging future. Pop may not have been typical of 1960s designs as a whole: but an appreciation of Pop does enable us to understand a good deal about the character and meaning of the more commonplace and everyday design of the 1960s.

A key role in shaping tastes and attitudes to design was played by the 'coloursupps', the symbol of Sixties publishing. The first was the *Sunday Times Colour Supplement* (later *Magazine*) and it began in February 1962. The *Telegraph Colour Supplement* followed in 1964; the *Observer Magazine* in 1965. All had a staple diet of art, fashion, design, consumer goods, travel and adventure which dovetailed perfectly with their glossy advertisements. One of the regular design features was the *Sunday Times Colour Supplement's* 'Design for Living' which commenced in April 1962 with an attack on decorum and 'good taste':

> 'Poor design has become a target for anyone with a brick to throw: good design is treated as a sort of sacred cow. The attitude to function is racing to the same level of absurdity; testing is turning into an obsession. There are times when one longs to buy something plumb ugly and utterly unfunctional.'[27]

Here was a point of view which undermined the basic premises bodies like the CoID had been pushing since the war. The 'coloursupps' promoted anything colourful, novel or even gimmicky so long as it had impact. With their liberal peppering of features on consumer goods and seductive advertisements for desirable hardware, the 'coloursupps' helped bring into currency the idea of young taste, trendiness and 'lifestyle'.

We can, in retrospect, recognise several iconological characteristics of 1960s design: fashionability; youthfulness; action and movement; modernity and progress; and starkness and unsentimentality. *Fashionability*—as we have already seen – is at the core of much Sixties design because it both expressed the mood of excitement, and satisfied the desires of a socially mobile and design-conscious public. Furthermore, by keeping turnover high, it was greeted with delight by manufacturers, retailers and designers. Fashionablenesss relied on impact, the inevitable corollary of which was small sustaining power, so guaranteeing a rapid turnover of styles. It was not any *one* style that mattered but the overall appearance and disappearance of styles – a constant change and expendability were signs that life was being lived to the full. Peter Murdoch's paper furniture was designed to last only as long as a pink paper dress and even then, physical expendability may have been overtaken by stylistic expendability. Particular makes and models of products became fashionable as the growing ranks of design *afficionados* advertised their cultural *connaissance* by possessing a *Braun* electric shaver, *Magistretti* chair or *Ronson* Escort 2000 hairdryer. A product's status was not necessarily dictated by its exclusiveness (in terms of cost), but its stylishness (in terms of 'designer' appeal). Richard Hamilton once perfectly summed up this knowing attitude. Writing of Dieter Rams' work for Braun, the artist declared that'...his consumer products have come to occupy the place in my heart and my consciousness that the Mont Saint-Victoire did in Cezanne's.'[29] Style-consciousness and style watching are now common pastimes but it is to the new-found affluent days of the colour-supplemented Sixties that their origins as mass phenomena can be traced.

The spirit of *youthfulness* percolated through much of the fashion and design. The decade felt itself to be young: 'Everyone wanted to look as though they were young, whether they were or weren't'[30] in Mary Quant's view. The colours and styles of clothes were both symbol and sign of youthfulness: symbol because of the connotations; sign because the styles made anyone over the age of 30 look anything from out-of-place to ridiculous. Nor, in retrospect, were the fashions liberal in their interpretation of youthful. Sixties youthfulness implied slim and sylph-like (Jean Shrimpton) or pre-pubescent and gangling (Twiggy). The early and mid-1960s were uncomplicated days. Anorexia was not yet a political issue and feminism gathered some pace only at the end of the decade. From the Carnaby Street 'dolly bird' to the pre-Raphaelitesque hippy, the young women conformed to what we now rightly see as quite blatantly sexist stereotypes.

The sort of youthfulness so apparent in fashion could also be seen in the colour, pattern and shape of furniture by such designers as Peter Murdoch and Bernard Holdaway in his Tom-o-tom range for Hull Traders. Even high street taste was influenced by youthful Pop colours. Strong primaries and secondaries filtered down from art via fashion and could be found on some television set casings and even refrigerators. The move towards significantly lower, back-aching seating (which culminated in scatter cushions) began in the Sixties, partly, one suspects, as a way of making life yet more difficult for the eardrum-beaten over 30s.

The imagery and, by extension *meaning* of youthfulness did, however, change during the decade. This is best illustrated by graphic design. 'Carnaby Street' imagery – Pop Art, Union Jacks, the space race *et al.* – connoted fun and frivolity. From late-1966 the hippy's psychedelic outlook and drug-induced consciousness-raising began to fragment youth culture. The imagery of psychedelia present – to those outside its cosmic circles – a decadent and, therefore, threatening lifestyle of radically alternative values. Carnaby Street could be accommodated in capitalism with ease: the hippy way of life was a rejection of capitalism itself. The major achievement of psychedelic graphics – in the work, for example, of Michael English and Martin Sharp – was to fuse form and content. *Oz* magazine included not only psychedelic graphics but incomprehensible and frequently illegible text. In the televisual, McLuhanesque age it was only the young who could fully understand that the *medium*, not the subject matter, was the message. And that message was 'Turn on, tune in and drop out.'

The hippies were a minority cult and few shared their world view. Most of the young just wanted a good time – and that involved *movement and action*.

15 Max Clendinning's 'Maxima' range for Race Furniture remains one of the best known examples of British Pop furniture.

Movement and action signified youthful, freedom from, and independence of, parental locations and constraints. With affluence the dream became a reality, facilitated by motorbikes, scooters and, increasingly, cars. Change was in the air as much as in the shops, so movement and action were necessary even if you were only going to stand still. Clothes were needed which both allowed and *expressed* freedom of movement. One magazine, enthralled with the space-race, called for '...space age clothes that can be launched to cram into suitcases, crush into narrow spaces for long journeys, and emerge at the end laboratory fresh.'[31] Life was hectic and a young girl needed clothes that could be put on '...first thing in the morning and still feel right at midnight; clothes that go happily to the office and equally happily out to dinner.'[32] Fashion photography changed accordingly. Replacing the formally-posed scenes of the 1950s in which models were unruffled, 1960s photography emphasised movement and surprise. In his autobiography Lord Snowdon (then Anthony Armstrong-Jones) remembers how he made the models '...run, dance, kiss – anything but stand still.'[33]

This was the age of the mini car as well as the mini dress. The Mini was a major break with traditional British car design and styling. Large British post-war cars were cumbersome and class-ridden, named after university towns and countryside retreats. Dashboards had a hint of arts and crafts about them. Small cars looked servile and aware of their place in society. The Mini was compact, efficient-looking, pared-down to basics and ready for active service. Its style and size made it look as if it belonged to the Sixties in the same way as did a mini-skirted girl. The other great symbol of movement and freedom was the transistor radio. As transistors became widely and cheaply available, the 'trannie' changed listening habits amongst the young. The image of the homogenous nuclear family huddled around the piece of furniture that was the wireless was as anachronistic as rationing. The 'trannie's' essential portability meant that the Pop fan need never be away from the top twenty, need never be aurally isolated in an alien environment of nature or silence. The styling of some transistor radios underlined their associations by borrowing the imagery of the walkie-talkie or the army combat radio. A whole range of objects was styled for youth on the move. One of the most remarkable was Ettore Sottsass' Valentine portable typewriter for Olivetti which, with its style-conscious form and bright red colour (with orange spools), looked more like a weekend case for the space-age *bon viveur* than a piece of mundane workaday equipment.

Movement and action signified change which in itself was seen as positive, a symptom of *modernity and progress.* Advances in science and technology were met with applause, and the space race – naively seen just in terms of man's quest to conquer the great unknown – won over the hearts of the public. The romance of technological progress was a key element of the sensibility of the 1960s, and the imagery of the space race infected many areas of design.

The new mood was put to great political effect by Harold Wilson as leader of the Labour Party. At his party's annual conference in 1963 Wilson outlined his vision of a progressive and classless Britain that would be '...forged in the white heat of the scientific revolution...'[34] Compared to the aristocratic and ageing Lord Home, the Conservative Prime Minister, Wilson appeared sprightly, energetic – even youthful. The electorate was on his side and after the '13 years of Tory misrule', Labour was returned to office in 1964 with a mandate – albeit a slender one – to change Britain from a conservative to a progressive nation. The period of the 'swinging Sixties' was a time of extravagant optimism when we seemed to be turning our backs on decades (if not centuries) of inequality and class warfare and embarking on a new age of classlessness and progress through advanced technology.

Design abounded with appearances and associations of modernity and progress. As well as the *imagery* taken from, for example, the space race and Pop or Op Art, *materials* and *forms* connoted the belief in the future. Plastics – whether injection-moulded furniture, disposable perspex jewellery, or PVC raincoats – were widely used. PVC clothes, for example, were produced in vivid colours, with decorative patterns, or were even transparent. But it was silver PVC, because of its associations with the astronaut's suit, that appeared the most space-age. As one excited fashion commentator exclaimed in 1965: silver clothing '...fits into current fashion like an astronaut into his capsule'[35]. PVC's significance, according to one designer, was that 'It's a material you can't work nostalgically, you have to make modern shapes.' The very texture and surface of PVC distanced it in time from conventional and *natural* materials, and located it in space.

Mainstream product design may have been less directly space-influenced, but it certainly sought to appear modern and up-to-date. Kenneth Grange's mid-1960s 'Kitchen Chef' for Kenwood, for example, exhibited the kind of solid simplicity and rigorous *gut form* which had previously been lacking in finnicky and fussy British design. Some so-called 'white goods' – washing machines and refrigerators – became the equal of their European counterparts. In personal product design and office hardware, the standards set by Braun, IBM and Olivetti were, to some extent, assimilated. These goods looked efficient, functional and business-like: fully a part of the modern world of corporate identities, corporation man and incorporated woman. In graphic design a similar rigour was apparent in the increasing amount of Constructivist-influenced work in magazines such as *Design* .

Form could also indicate the image of modernity. On the one hand innovative forms such as the small-wheeled Moulton bicycle or Max Clendinning's sculpturally-influenced 'Maxima' range of furniture were progressive because they broke radical conventions. Less innovative forms also appeared very modern when they exploited materials and colour in a certain way. Kenneth Grange's 1968 'Egg' lighter is a case in point. This object epitomised three traits of a strand of later-1960s design. First, although it is sophisticated in finish and warm in tactile quality, the *material* is not seeking to be anything other than that archetypally Sixties material, plastic. Second, it is white, a 'colour' associated primarily with space and, by extension, hygiene, efficiency, purity and clarity – the 'I'm-all-white, wack' look was popularised by John Lennon in his quest for spiritual honesty. Third, the *form* has the bottom-heavy, rather weighty proportions visible in much plastics design, especially the furniture of the time. Such forms may have been facilitated by the characteristics of plastic as a material and the technique of injection-moulding, but it was more than technological determinism which accounts for the heavy shape. In the particular instance of the 'Egg' lighter, the Pop sensibility and wit of using the inappropriate and incongruous image of an egg for a lighter obviously appealed to Grange,

16 One of a series of table lighters which Kenneth Grange designed for Ronson. In each case the mechanism was already provided, and Grange's task was to design the housing. For the 'Egg Table Lighter' he chose 'an egg - a familiar, ever beautiful form, which gave a touch of humour without risking absurdity.'

but the proportions of the object evoke a whole period. The rounded forms are to the later 1960s what rectilinear forms were to the 1920s and streamlined shape to the 1930s. All signify modernity but with different associations. The rectilinear style referred to industrial mass-production and the machine; streamlining to fast movement through water and air; the rounded shape to structural strength, completeness and perfection. Rounded, continuous forms look like technology in a futuristic state. Emphasis is no longer given to the rational and logical industrial processes of production (as it had been with Modernist design) but to a *gestalt* form which seems to have been as mysteriously conceived and magically produced as a seamless gown. (The influence of Eastern religions, with their various uses of the circle as a symbol, was strong at the time). These rather mannerist formal tendencies are what now gives this style of 1960s design such a dated appearance.

The widespread use of *undisguised* synthetic materials, the novel shapes and forms and the absence of historicist or traditional ornament and decoration underlined just how much the 1960s was, at the time, viewed as a break with the past. This feeling was particularly virulent in Britain because of the weight accorded to tradition and heritage. The British have found it hard – as we can so clearly witness today – to fully commit themselves to the present, preferring instead to hark nostalgically and sentimentally back to 'the past'. This *attitude* to the present (which is revealed by the mythology of the past) was one of the main battlefields in the 1960s. The new attitude was often unambiguously *unsentimental* and it was frequently manifested by a visual *starkness*. Both these

29

aspects can be observed in the portrait photography of the time. David Bailey's *Box of Pin Ups* (1965), his selection of portraits of the models, pop singers, artists, hairdressers, tycoons and even criminals who composed 'the scene', is the apotheosis of the attitude. The sitters are portrayed in the glare of harsh lighting, not as individual human beings with complex emotional personalities but as objects who are but images. This accords with the presentation of celebrities in the televisual age: we may think we know a person well through media exposure, but we see the person only from the outside and only as an image. Bailey's portraits reveal not the sitter's inner state but his/her outer image. These photographs are not manipulated by Bailey in the sense that he wishes to make a moral point, they merely reflect the dehumanised, unsentimental, emotional starkness that became fashionable in certain circles. Much fashion photography followed suit with models expressing a visage of detachment and inscrutability.

But it is in architecture where starkness and unsentimentality tell us so much about the decade. The layman's view of architecture in the 1960s was that it was inhumane. The mistrust in and lack of respect for architects is a legacy we are still having to cope with. The symbol of Sixties architecture is the high-rise dwelling block flanked by an expressway. This was the response to two major problems which we should not underestimate. First was the need for new housing, the result of a sharp increase in the population, and the demise into squalor – exacerbated by the war – of poor mid-Victorian housing stock. Aspirations were, of course, also changing and, by the early 1960s, young couples showed less willingness to accept the substandard conditions endured by their parents. Second was the need for a road network in keeping with the third quarter of the Twentieth century. This could only be comprehensively carried out by sweeping away whole streets and, occasionally, whole areas, so adding to the housing problem. Such change could only be carried out in a determined way in an age of confidence when there was a full-blooded belief in progress. The characters of countless towns and cities were transformed during this era of wholesale demolition and rebuilding. What people noticed most was that the *scale* of their environs had changed. The pre-1960s Britain had been designed on a scale to which the individual could relate: 1960s Britain was being built to a scale by which the individual was overwhelmed. High-rise is the obvious example. The Victorian terraced house was designed around a grouping of individuals – the family – and each house gave direct access to the community of the street as well as allowing individuals to announce their presence by, for example, their choice of coloured paintwork. By contrast, high-rise seemed to work on the level of only the amorphous 'mass'; in spite of (or, rather, because of) the street-in-the-air concept, access to the community was closed off; and individuals had little opportunity to express anything other than their frustration and resentment. To a British public aspiring to home ownership, the forms and groupings of high-rise blocks were as culturally alien as they were socially alienating.

There was an equally great gap between the public's and architects' taste when it came to materials. The architects' favoured building material was raw concrete – a material as loved by architects as it was loathed by the public for its rough-hewn, gutsy and anti-picturesque qualities. Furthermore, its poor weathering properties and consequent unsuitability to the British climate did not endear it to the daily users of the buildings. The two complexes which symbolise

17 The image of people stacked one above the other in boxes, with a facade presenting endless dull conformity, is apparent in many blocks of flats, especially those using the new prefabricated systems on the market in the Sixties.

18 The 'Brutalist' concrete of London's much-derided South Bank complex would seem a strange choice of location for a photograph of Mary Quant's Ginger Group fashions. But there was much in common between assertive architecture and fashions to look good, though often at the expense of comfort. *Petticoat* magazine, March 1968.

this (significantly named) Brutalist movement are the Hayward Gallery on London's South Bank, and the Hyde Park housing development in Sheffield. From the perspective of the present, their brutal(ist) starkness appears uncaring and inhumane in its unsentimentality. And herein lies the essential difference between the 1960s and today. We may be understandably nostalgic for the feeling of optimism which percolated through most of the decade. We may even admire the willingness and determination to tackle problems like housing with such resolve and confidence (while we should acknowledge the element of self-glorification in politicians', planners' and architects' motives). But we cannot empathise with the visions because we no longer share the certain belief in an essentially Modernist future with its ideology of technological progressivism.

The shift in sensibility that dominates the third phase of the Sixties begins in about 1967. The young who had voted Labour in 1964 and again in 1966 in the belief that society would be transformed, had become at first disillusioned and then angry. The Labour administration, they declared, had been a Tory government run by Labour politicians. The political system merely maintained the obscene status quo. Radical politics were necessary, and direct and bloody action was inevitable. In architecture, the collapse of the Ronan Point tower block in London in 1968 drew sensational attention to the widespread unpopularity of high-rise living and the woefully inadequate level of research and testing on prefabricated systems of building. Architects suddenly found they were being held responsible for the social unhappiness associated with the high-rise idea, and that they had lost the confidence of the public at large. Planners were blamed for turning the inner city into a concrete desert. Professionals of all kinds came under fire.

Designers responded with a changing outlook. In 1967 in *Design*, J. Christopher Jones urged designers to look at the wider issues and study the environmental effects of products.[37] Pollution, conservation and the destruction of the countryside were all subjects with which, Jones argued, the designer should concern himself. Socially responsible thinking gathered momentum. The tone of this post-1966 period was captured by Michael Middleton in an article in *The Designer* in 1970 called 'The Wider Issues at Stake'. Middleton wrote of '...a movement of public opinion, a developing concern, which is one of the genuinely hopeful events of the decade.' He continued with an explanation that

'What is hopeful is that the wider public is now beginning to grasp the scale, the complexity, the interlocking nature of such problems. What is at stake is nothing less than the quality of life itself – not in a century's time, but twenty, ten, two year's time.'[38]

The concerns to which Middleton referred included the Torrey Canyon oil slick, the Aberfan slag heap disaster, traffic congestion in city and town centres, speculative property development, and air and water pollution. A forceful environmentalist lobby was growing which expressed concern about the stagnation of rivers, the pollution of air and the noise of aeroplanes. A proposed

1 The ultimate symbol of the disposable ethic, paper funiture was, however, surprisingly strong. The apparent simplicity of this child's chair by Peter Murdoch belies its extremely complex development.

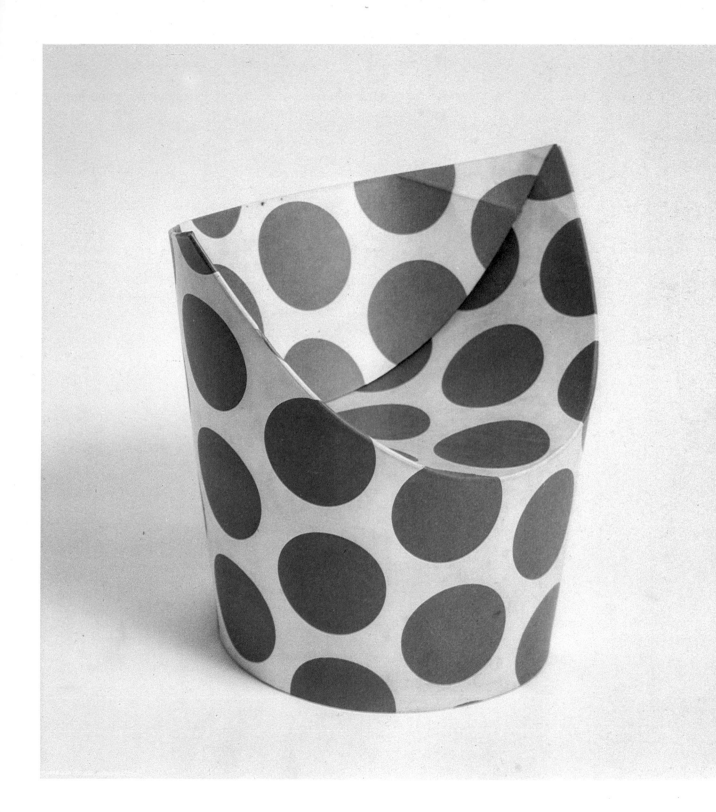

11 Martin Sharp designed the front cover for issue no. 3 of Oz magazine; the name of the magazine is almost lost in the graphic decoration.

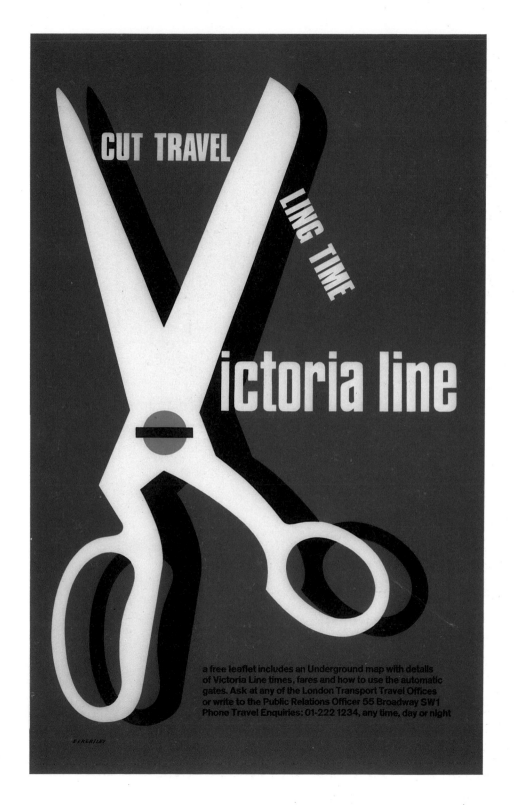

CUT TRAVEL

LING TIME

Victoria line

a free leaflet includes an Underground map with details
of Victoria Line times, fares and how to use the automatic
gates. Ask at any of the London Transport Travel Offices
or write to the Public Relations Officer 55 Broadway SW1
Phone Travel Enquiries: 01-222 1234, any time, day or night

ECKERSLEY

III This poster, designed by Tom Eckersley
for London Transport in 1969 for the
opening of the new Victoria Line, was
surprisingly traditional, looking back to the
hand drawn, fine art traditions of McKnight
Kauffer rather than to the newer
photographic styles which one might have
thought more suited to such a project.

IV One of the earliest examples of the use of rural imagery which has since become a popular way of selling foodstuffs; Wolff Olins's romanticised image of the pieman maintains a carefully controlled balance between the 'real' (photographic) and 'fantasy' (hand drawn) elements. Rural imagery, located in an unspecific past, provides associations with 'traditional' cooking methods, as well as implying freshness by the bright green of the landscape.

V Wolff Olins chose the colour red for BOC's corporate image because of its associations with strength and aggressiveness. It also has, as the designer's brochure stated, 'a strong after image effect…you continue to see it in your mind's eye even after it has passed from sight.' The use of stripes, a conventional warning symbol, is another way of demanding attention for the company.

Hadfields
Acrylic Gloss
paint

sorry closed

Previous page

VI As a symbol for Hadfields Gloss Paint, Wolff
Olins chose a fox, which is shown running,
jumping, curling up and sleeping, on headed
letter paper, paint cans, factories and delivery
vans. The fox bore no relation to Hadfield's
products; the designers claimed it represented 'a
firm living by its wits in a consumer world'.

VII Victorian and Edwardian styles enjoyed a
popular revival from the mid to late Sixties. This
printed cotton furnishing fabric, 'Petrus' by Peter
Hall for Heal's, employs the flat stylised floral
motifs with outlined details characteristic of Art
Nouveau.

VIII Of all the technological advances of the
Sixties none caught the imagination more than
those made in space travel. The landing of the
first men on the moon in 1969 was the inspiration
behind this design called 'Lunar Rocket' by Eddie
Squires for Warner's, the textile manufacturer.

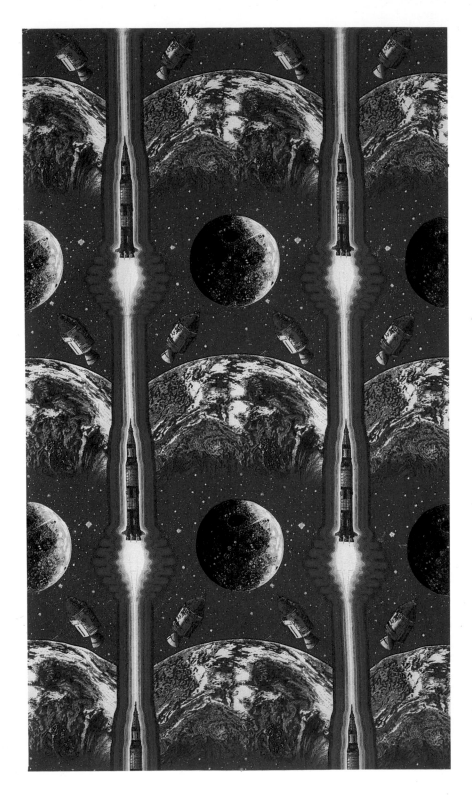

IX 'Hecuba', a
wallpaper designed by
David Bartle for
Sanderson's 1968
Palladio 8 collection,
with screenprinted
colours covered by a
vinyl protective surface.
Paper-backed vinyl
wallcoverings were
introduced into Britain by
ICI in 1962, with their
'Vymura' range.
Although more
expensive than
conventional wallpapers,
vinyl papers lasted
longer and were easier
to clean, and therefore
soon became popular.

X   Susan Burgess-James's 'Lombard' wallpaper designed in 1968 for the Crown 'Cleenstrip' Collection; an example to the late Sixties revival of interest in Art Deco designs.

third London airport was (at that time) successfully opposed on environmental and ecological grounds. Within two or three years the concerns of a minority of long-haired radicals and hippies had become major issues for the professional classes. The practical and psychological effects of the energy crisis compounded the loss of faith in the shining new future that had been forecast in the 1960s. The 'swinging Sixties' had become history.

Nigel Whiteley Ph.D., FRSA, is head of the Department of Visual Arts, University of Lancaster.

Notes

1. See Arthur Marwick, *Britain in Our Century* London 1984, p 167
2. See Central Statistical Office (CSO) *Social Trends* number 10, 1978. Table 10.14, p 64
3. ibid fig A.23
4. Spoken on 'Tonic to the Nation?' BBC Radio 4 29 November 1976
5. Michael Farr, *Design in British Industry*, London 1955, p xxxvi
6. ibid p 52
7. ibid p xxxxvi
8. Editor, 'The basis of Choice', *Design* August 1962, p 23
9. John E. Blake, 'The Case for Criticism', *Design* June 1961, p 43
10. Reyner Banham, 'H.M. Fashion House', *New Statesman* 27 January 1961, p 51
11. ibid p 151
12. For a selection of Banham's writings see Penny Sparke (ed), *Reyner Banham: Design by Choice*, London 1981
13. Herbert Read, *Art and Industry*, London 1934, 1966 edn., p 17
14. Misha Black, 'Taste, Style and Industrial Design', *Motif* number 4, 1960, p 63
15. Peter Lewis, *The Fifties*, London 1978, p 118
16. Quoted by Georgina Howell, *In Vogue*, London 1975, p 278
17. Editor, *The Times*, leader article, quoted by Bernard Levin, *The Pendulum Years*, London 1970, p 66
18. Ernestine Carter, 'The Year in Fashion', *Sunday Times Magazine*, 29 December 1963 p 31
19. Mary Quant, *Quant by Quant*, London 1966 p 73
20. Quoted by Barbara Barnard, *Fashion in the 60s*, London 1978, p 16
21. Quoted in anon, 'The Year of the Crunch – The Challengers' *Queen*, 2 January 1963, p 6
22. Editor, *Tailor and Cutter*, 21 February 1964, p 226
23. Editor, *Tailor and Cutter*, 13 December 1963, p 1733
24. Editor, *Tailor and Cutter*, 27 January 1967, p 98
25. Barbara Griggs, 'Fashion on the Boil', *Harpers Bazaar*, February 1965, p 66
26. Ken and Kate Baynes, 'Behind the Scene', *Design*, August 1966, p 28
27. Janice Elliott, 'Design-Function', *Sunday Times Magazine*, 15 April 1962, p 26
28. Quoted by Polly Derlin, 'The Furniture Designer Who Became a Reluctant Businessman', *House and Garden*, November 1964, p 78
29. Richard Hamilton, 'The Braun Paintings' in Francois Burkhardt and Inez Franksen (eds), *Design: Dieter Rams Et*, Berlin 1981, p 183
30. Mary Quant, 'A Personal Design for Living', *The Listener*, 19/26 December 1974, p 816
31. anon, 'Clothes in a Go Condition', *Vogue*, May 1962, p 120
32. Mary Quant, *Quant by Quant*, London 1966, p110
33. Quoted in, *The Sunday Times Magazine*, 9 December 1979, p 29
34. Harold Wilson, 'Labour and the Scientific Revolution', *Labour: Annual Conference Report* 1963, p 140
35. anon, 'Steel in', *Queen*, 14 July 1965, p 59
36. Sally Jess quoted by Meriel McCooey, 'Plastic Bombs', *The Sunday Times Magazine*, 15 August 1965, p 27
37. J. Christopher Jones, 'Trying to Design the Future', *Design*, September 1967, pp 35-39
38. Michael Middleton, 'The Wider Issues at Stake', *The Designer*, February 1970, p 1.

Battle of Hastings 1066

HARRISON AND SONS LTD

4d

19 British stamp design underwent a drastic improvement in the mid-Sixties. The eight stamps in this issue, designed by David Gentleman, formed a continuous strip which echoed the original source, the Bayeux Tapestry. 900 years free from invasion was something to celebrate at a time when people were looking resolutely to the future.

1966: A YEAR IN FOCUS

From the standpoint of 1986 it is particularly tempting to look back on 1966 through rose-coloured spectacles. With spiralling unemployment and few British sporting triumphs to lighten our mood, a certain amount of nostalgia seems excusable when looking back twenty years. 1966 was a year of record low levels of unemployment. Wages had, over the previous six years, increased at almost double the rate of prices. It was, of course, the year England won the World Cup. Many will also think of 1966 as the year in which the Labour Party was returned to power with a huge majority, committed to a future of social equality, and of the careful husbanding of technological improvements to produce increased wealth for everyone. It is not only nostalgia which produces the rosy tones; a celebratory note was sounded at the time too, with the 'swinging Sixties' craze of 1965 spilling over into the following year, mingling with the Union Jack souvenirs of the England team's World cup triumph. Guinness ran an advertising campaign with the motto 'Battle of Hastings 1066 – Bottle of Guinness 1966', which seemed to imply that, even if the score had been France 1 – England 0 in the 11th century, England had nevertheless won the return match. The Union Jack was also much in evidence when Francis Chichester set out on his lone voyage around the world on 27 August 1966.

This is, of course, not the whole story, and not only because events such as the October Aberfan disaster have been omitted is this a misleading account of the year. In many areas of life, but particularly in the political, economic and social fields, there is evidence of a sense of unease developing during 1966, a feeling that the 'bubble of confidence' was about to burst. We have chosen to focus our study of the Sixties around 1966 because, with hindsight, it is possible to see this year as a turning point in the decade which was more significant than any developments which took place as 1959 became 1960. As Nigel Whiteley has shown (see p 13) in so many areas of design, work produced in the years leading up to 1966 differs strongly from that produced during the rest of the decade. There is clearly no simple, causal relationship between social and economic change, and developments in design, but if we accept Adrian Forty's contention that design has the power to cast ideas and beliefs about our lives into material form,[1] then we must evidently make some attempt to understand the nature of

BATTLE OF HASTINGS 1066

BOTTLE OF GUINNESS 1966

20 A witty poster for Guinness, which won the CoID's British Poster Design Awards in 1966; the judging panel considered it an 'entertaining use of a transient event'.

those significant changes which seem so clearly to separate the last three years of the decade from the first six.

It now seems clear that the most important, in terms of far-reaching effects, of the changes taking place in Britain during 1966, occurred in the economic and political arenas. Although, on 31 March, voters had increased Labour's 1964 election majority to a resounding 100, the evidence of the ballot box partially obscured the growing dissatisfaction with which many groups of people were coming to view the government's performance. This dissatisfaction seems to have begun, even before the election, amongst both traditional Fabian and younger, more left-wing, middle-class party members, many of whom were totally disillusioned by the support which Harold Wilson gave to the United States' bombing of North Vietnam in February 1965, and who were shocked by the apparent racism of the government's decision, later that year, to cut by over half the annual number of work permits issued to Commonwealth citizens.

It seems likely that Labour's 1966 election majority was largely due to the continued support of large sections of the industrial working class, but, before the year was out, this too had been substantially eroded. There were two main reasons for this. The first was Wilson's attack on the seamen's strike, which began in May, the leaders of which he accused of being Trotskyites. When this was followed a few months later by a rise in prescription charges and the abolition of free school milk in secondary schools, it seemed that the very cornerstone of socialist policy, the Welfare State, was under attack from a Labour Government. By November 1966, the 15 percent lead that Labour had gained over the Tories in the May opinion polls, had been reduced to nothing.

More crucial, however, than any of these developments, was the economic crisis of 1966. As a result of the seamen's strike, there was a run on the pound which forced the government to introduce, on 20 July, a stringent package of deflationary measures: cuts in public spending, a credit squeeze, and a wages and prices freeze. For many people these measures seemed to mark the end of the 'boom years'.

A Gallup opinion poll published in May 1966 claimed that 46 percent of the population thought that it was important for Britain to be a world power. No doubt this sort of thinking lay behind the Labour government's unwillingness, at this stage, to devalue the pound. The run on the pound had demonstrated growing recognition abroad of the fact that Britain was living beyond its means. The *Observer* called the 20 July 'The Day it all stopped'. A *New York Times* reporter writing on 8 June about the seamen's strike had sensed an impending crisis: 'The atmosphere in London', he wrote, 'can almost be eerie in its quality of relentless frivolity. There can rarely have been a greater contrast between a country's objective situation and the mood of its people.' *The Sunday Times* in August concluded that 'The Age of Pop' was 'Swinging to a Stop' ... 'now the revolution seems to have spent its force.'

In social terms, it is amongst the young that 1966 seems to mark the most striking turning point of all. Associations of 'youthfulness' had been useful both to the press celebrating the 'vitality' of 'swinging London' and to politicians pursuing a more modern, innovative and affluent society. Up until 1966 'youthful rebellion' had mainly taken forms that 'the Establishment' had not had too much difficulty in manipulating. After 1966, this was no longer the case.

In 1967, the largely US based hippy cult crossed the Atlantic. For many of its mainly middle-class following this involved a complete rejection of existing British society, and the creation of an 'alternative' way of life. There were various groupings within the hippy movement, some of whose members were more interested in political activism, than in drugs and psychedelia, but neither aspect could be easily defused by the existing British Establishment.

Equally important were divisions occurring amongst young Britons themselves. Although there can have been few middle-class youths, male or female, not in some way affected by the hippy cult, working-class youths remained largely unimpressed. Even before 1966, many working-class youths, of both sexes, had been attracted to the short cropped hair, sharp clothes, and 'ska' music taken up by young West Indians in Britain, who liked the connection the style gave them with Jamaica. By 1966 'rocksteady' music had developed as the focus of a viable alternative movement for working-class white and black youths who disliked the

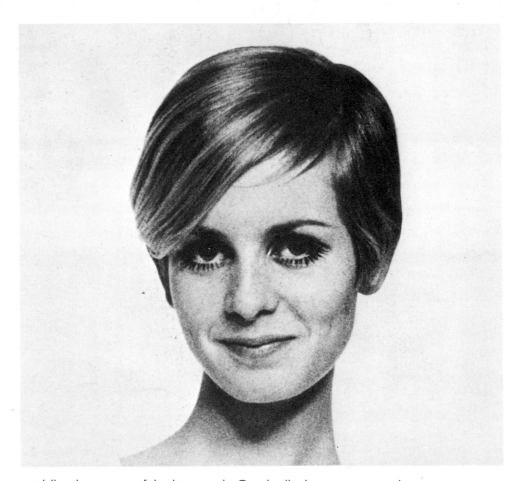

21 Seventeen-year-old Twiggy was introduced as 'The Face of '66' by the *Daily Express;* within a few months she was Britain's most sought-after model, and by the end of 1966 she was voted 'Woman of the Year'.

middle-class aura of the hippy cult. Gradually, however, even the apparent unity of this subsection of youth culture began to crumble as the growth of rastafarianism amongst its black members caused tension between them and some of the whites.

Thus, by 1966, there were already signs not only of an impending split, more serious than anything seen during the early Sixties, between youth and the Establishment in Britain, but also of serious divisions amongst young Britons themselves, for the most part along broadly class-based lines. These divisions, as well as the economic and political developments discussed earlier, were ignored by certain members of the press who continued to present London as the 'swinging' capital of a country in which the vitality and new 'classlessness' of its young were well represented by the commercial successes of David Bailey, Michael Caine and Twiggy. By November of 1967, however, the financial crisis of 1966 had culminated in the devaluation of the pound; another nail in the coffin of swinging and prosperous 'Great' Britain.

Notes
1. Adrian Forty, *Objects of Desire: Design and Society 1750-1980*, London 1986, p9

22 1966 has been described as 'the craziest fashion year of the sixties'. Almost all designers were infected by the notion of 'space age fashion', and plastic was the most fashionable material. This outfit was selected as Bath Museum of Costume's 'Dress of the Year'.

INDEX OF PRICES, WAGES AND PROFITS

DATE	RETAIL PRICES	WEEKLY WAGES	COMPANY PROFITS
1960	100	100	100
1961	103	108	100
1962	108	113	103
1963	110	118	120
1964	113	127	138
1965	119	141	145
1966	124	154	137
1967	127	159	145
1968	133	172	166
1969	140	185	171

1966: THE SHOPPING BASKET

Bread: large white, 28 oz	1s 3½d	(6p)
small white, 14 oz	9d	(4p)
1 dozen eggs	3s 10d	(19p)
1lb English butter	4s 5d	(22p)
2 lb packet sugar	1s 5d	(7p)
1 pint beer	1s 7½d	(8½p)
1 bottle whiskey	£2 8s 6d	(2.42½p)
20 king size cigarettes	5s 4d	(27p)
1 gallon 4 star petrol	5s 2½d	(26p)

(Grocery prices are national averages taken from *Which?* Magazine's survey, September 1966)

1966: THE CONSUMER

a) **Secondary school teacher** – basic salary £730 pa. Rising to £1,400 p.a. with 14 years' experience. Grant for teacher training £170 pa.

b) **Student –** London, Oxford or Cambridge – £420 pa. Elsewhere – £305 pa. Number of students: London, Oxford, Cambridge – 63,381 Other sectors – 206,241

c) **Unemployed –** Over 18 – £4 p.w. (i.e. £208 pa). Under 18 – £25s 6d pw. Women – £2 15s pw.

d) **Car assembly line worker** – £21 pw (ie £1,092 pa).

e) **General Practitioner average** – £4,000 pa.

f) **Supermarket cashier, female** – £10 for a 40 hour week (ie £520 pa).

1966: Average weekly earnings for male manual worker £20 11s 0d Deduction for a married man with one child under 11 and a wife not working: Tax £2 1s 0d National Insurance £1 1s 6d Total deductions £3 2s 6d Net average weekly earnings: £17 8s 8d

Employment figures June 1966: 25,620,000 employed; 16,640,000 males and 8,980,000 females June 1966: 253,000 unemployed November 1966: 543,000 unemployed Number of strikes during 1966: 1,930 involving 542,000 workers: 2,392,000 days lost.

1966: CHRONOLOGY

January
17 – U.S. hydrogen bomb is lost over Spain; recovered 7 April
19 – Mrs Ghandi becomes Prime Minister of India
31 – Ban on trade with Rhodesia
– U.S. resumes bombing of North Vietnam

February
3 – Soviet spacecraft Luna, soft landing on the moon
22 – UK defence estimates. £2,172m
23 – UK Budget estimate, £7,728m

March
31 – Labour win General Election, 100 majority

April
5 – Shell/Esso, major North Sea gas find
19 – 'Moors' murder trial opens

May
3 – Budget day
– *The Times* begins to print news on the front page
16 – Seamen's strike begins, lasts until 2 July
– Unemployment at a record low

July
3 – Anthony Wedgwood-Benn appointed new Minister of Technology
20 – Wages and prices standstill
– Ian Paisley imprisoned – riots in Ulster
30 – World Cup Final – England beat West Germany 4-2

August
27 – Francis Chichester begins his solo round the world voyage

September
6 – Dr. Voerword, South African President, assassinated in Cape Town
8 – Cost of Concorde had escalated to £500m
– Severn Bridge opened
15 – First Polaris submarine launched

October
21 – Aberfan disaster, 116 children killed

November
10 – Government announces its intention to join the E.E.C.
22 – White Paper – Price and Incomes standstill

December
2 – Harold Wilson and Ian Smith discuss the future of Rhodesia on HMS Tiger off Gibraltar
12 – White Paper proposes decimalization of British currency by 1970
25 – 158 die on the roads at Christmas.

23 The Sainsbury interior was
designed to be light, clean, and
spacious, with point of sale
advertisements kept to a minimum.
Sainsbury's 'good design' approach
worked well in commercial terms: they
had the highest turnover per square
foot of any supermarket.

NEW TRENDS IN SHOPPING AND SELLING

A NEW LOOK FOR THE HIGH STREET

In 1960, retailing in Britain stood on the threshold of a new age: increasing affluence, coupled with a growing sophistication in merchandising, was set to change the face of the High Street irrevocably. It was not so much the newcomers to the shopping scene such as the boutique, the betting shop and the fast food outlet that changed things, but the the considerable advances made by two developments which had been apparent for a number of years. The first was the growth of self service: in restaurants, supermarkets or petrol stations. As the Chairman of Unilever explained in 1965, this meant a radical rethink about advertising and packaging: 'If your goods' he wrote 'are to be sold by self service, your package is fighting for you against every other package.'[1]

The other main trend was towards rationalisation and concentration: from small independent shops to chain stores. Statistically the share of the market controlled by the independents dropped from 54.2 to 46.5 percent between 1961-70, whilst that of the multiples grew from 28 to 36.8 percent[2] As clearance schemes in residential and central areas demolished the old corner shops, they were replaced by larger units concentrated into precincts and shopping malls. This trend was reinforced by the removal of Resale Price Maintenance; large shops were able to offer savings which the smaller outlets could not compete with. The increasing dominance of the market by chains such as Smith's, Boots, and Marks and Spencer's and the various supermarket and bank chains, meant that every reasonably sized town in Britain began to present much the same appearance. The development of distinctive and consistent 'house styles' such as the clean, rational, if rather old fashioned, approach of Marks and Spencer's meant that when you entered one of their shops, wherever it was in Britain, the effect was reassuringly the same.

THE RISE OF THE SUPERMARKET

Supermarket shopping, with its roots in the earlier American consumer boom, became one of the most potent symbols of affluence in the Sixties; there were 2,500 supermarkets in 1966 compared with 367 in 1960. Because many of these

24 The point of sale area in Sainsbury's supermarket in Feltham in 1966.

new supermarkets were located in out-of-town and suburban locations so that they could provide adequate parking facilities, the association with affluence was reinforced. Supermarkets concentrated on a high turnover of low unit cost merchandise, with prices lower than in traditional shops. Merchandise was displayed *en masse*, on the stepped shelves that were known in the trade as gondolas, or in large freezer cabinets. The store and the display were laid out for easy access, and designed for self-service. The goods themselves were packaged in a range of new materials, making use of new techniques, to ensure freshness and visibility.

Sainsbury's

Whilst supermarkets in general often followed the hard sell approach of their American antecedents and showed little design sensitivity, one company, Sainsbury's, stood out. They set up their own design studio, and the house style they developed was decisive in carrying over a reputation for cleanliness and

25　The rise in importance of the supermarket went hand in hand with the development of own brand goods. Sainsbury's were particularly successful in producing an easily recognisable house packaging style which made their goods stand out from the brasher approach of the household names.

26　The first Biba boutique was opened in Abingdon Road, Kensington, in 1964. The shop had formerly been a chemist's, and Barbara Hulanicki and her friends re-decorated it themselves with black and white floor tiles, walls painted in navy blue, and the curtains in a plum and navy William Morris print. The furnishings were mostly second-hand.

value for money, from their traditional stores, into their new supermarkets. A recognisable packaging style was particularly important, as Sainsbury's, like many of the other chains, put increased emphasis on the production of their own brand goods. Brand goods could certainly compete in price with the heavily advertised household names, but they needed to be easily distinguishable in the store. In the early days all that was needed to make them stand out was a pure design approach in which white dominated; but the style gradually developed greater impact, with a general movement from graphic to photographically based designs. John Sainsbury summed up the company's policy: 'We expect our design to be clean and clear and straightforward and – most important – to contribute a mark of quality to all products bearing our label'.[3] Applied to the store in general, this policy produced clean, spacious layouts, severely limited point of sale advertising and an architectural style which used materials such as mosaic and tiles. From the fascia to the paper bag, the Sainsbury's motif, in an easily recognisable typeface, was the guarantee of quality that the company was aiming for.

THE RISE OF THE BOUTIQUE

At a time when shopping was becoming less personalised, and stores were losing their individuality, the phenomenon of the boutique arose as a symbol of the youthful, creative, entrepreneurial spirit. Mary Quant's Bazaar opened in King's Road, Chelsea, in 1955, and John Stephen opened the first of his many shops in Carnaby Street four years later. Not much older than their first customers, they were successful because they identified a market which the larger manufacturers were only inadequately serving. The irresistible rise of the boutique in the Sixties occurred in response to the demand for specifically young

27 The familiar daisy motif remains a witness to Mary Quant's success in emphasising, through a bold graphic device, the associations of excitement and modernity which she wanted her clothes to create.

fashions from the newly-affluent under-25s. By 1970 the *Daily Mail* estimated that there were some 15,000 boutiques spread across the country, catering mainly for this age group.[4]

Ken and Kate Baynes in *Design* magazine in 1966 identified three main categories of boutique: those owned by designer manufacturers; those owned by semi-amateurs, often set up with limited capital and employing a few machinists; and the specialist shop within a large store[5]. The latter, which attempted to reproduce the boutique scale and their selling methods, were, perhaps unknowingly, reviving the boutique in its original sense (much earlier in the century, the boutique had been a shop within a couture house, and only later came to mean a small, exclusive clothes shop). The boutique aimed at an ever-changing and rapid turnover of stock. As a result work could not be done by the traditional big manufacturers whose production methods were geared to seasonal collections, with long runs of individual styles and programmed delivery dates. For the kind of high-speed production of small quantities which the boutiques required the work was usually sent to outworkers.

28 When, in 1968, Biba began selling clothes nationally by mail order, John McConnell was asked to design the graphics for their catalogues and other stationery which would convey the associations and ideas which, for London customers, were provided by the interior design of the shop.

The boutique environment was as different from that in traditional clothes shops as were the clothes on sale. Compared with the formality and intimidating atmosphere of the latter, the boutique used pop music to create an exciting ambience, the staff were young, and you could try on as many clothes as you liked, without feeling reproached if you did not buy. Boutique owners frequently claimed that they were selling the sort of clothes which they themselves wore. The traffic was two-way, since the scale and intimacy of most of the shops allowed rapid feedback of fashion trends from customer to owner. Thus, boutique fashion may be seen as being created essentially by the consumer, and thence finding its way into the mainstream via shops which attempted to sell back to the consumer his or her ideals of youthfulness and belonging.

Bazaar and Biba

The essence of the boutique approach to selling was to make shopping enjoyable, and from the very outset Mary Quant's Bazaar aimed to promote this idea. The physical location of the shop helped, since Bazaar was above a basement restaurant and late opening allowed people to come in and buy clothes after an evening meal. The 'fun' element was also emphasised through window displays constructed with the primary aim of entertaining, even shocking, passers-by, and through such extravagances as giving away hundreds of pounds' worth of lollipops to children at Christmas.

Quant described the atmosphere at Bazaar as 'a sort of permanently running cocktail party',[6] a description which nicely emphasises the social class of the market at which her clothes were initially aimed. Although she considered the price of her clothes to be 'cheap', this was true only in comparison with the products of the couture houses, alongside which they were displayed at fashion shows. In comparison with, for example, clothes sold at Biba, they were expensive. The comparison is important; Mary Quant's clothes designs, although considered outrageous at first, were relatively quickly given 'official' approval whereas, as Barbara Hulanicki wrote of Biba, 'the glossy establishment press never took us seriously. We were just a gimmick...'[7]

The differing social and financial backgrounds of Mary Quant and Barbara Hulanicki affected not only the kind of customer each attracted, but also the marketing methods they used. Barbara Hulanicki lacked the financial backing that had enabled Quant to open a shop very early in her career, and so, initially, the clothes she designed were sold by mail order. In this way, money received with customers' orders could be used to buy materials and pay for labour costs, before the clothes were sent out.

The first Biba boutique opened in Abingdon Road, Kensington in 1964 and, from the outset, its appeal was quite different from that of Bazaar. With windows which let in very little light, it relied on creating an air of mystery and exoticism through which to sell clothes. The atmosphere was re-created in a second shop, opened in Kensington Church Street in March 1966, which had a 'bordello' changing room with scarlet walls, deep red carpet, gilt mirrors, and china pedestal jardinières.

In the most successful boutiques, careful attention was paid to the design of graphics and packaging as well as to the interior decoration of the shop. When

29   In September 1969 Biba moved
to a larger building in Kensington
High Street. The 'art deco' style of the
new building provided a different
atmosphere for the shop, which was
reflected in a new graphic design
style. The essential function of the
style, of conjuring up the imagined
luxury and romance of an age now
past, remained the same.

Mary Quant decided to go into mass production, with her 'Ginger Group' label
in 1963, she was anxious to maintain the same air of 'specialness', if not outright
exclusivity, which had characterised the clothes on sale in Bazaar. This she
achieved by keeping a tight control over the graphic style with which her goods
were presented and sold in other shops. Hulanicki also relied on the consistent
use of strong graphic motifs. In her case, their function was to ensure that the
association of her clothes with some unspecified and exotic past was maintained
throughout the sales process. The need for a unifying graphic style was, as might

30 A carrier bag from the Manchester Habitat which opened in 1967. The image and the lettering are in red against a yellow ground. The bright colours conveyed a sense of excitement, whilst the choice of objects depicted and the style of drawing had a 'continental' air.

be expected, felt most strongly at a time when the business was expanding, to avoid the possible 'watering down' of the style associated with Biba.

'PRE-DIGESTED SHOPPING' : HABITAT

When Terence Conran announced the opening of the first Habitat shop in 1964 he expressed the hope that he had 'taken the foot-slogging out of shopping by assembling a wide selection of unusual and top quality goods under one roof'.[8] He described Habitat as offering the consumer a 'pre-digested shopping programme';[9] in other words, he was selling furniture and accessories that made up a coherent style, and he had a specific audience in mind for that style.

Conran's was by no means the first attempt to offer shopping facilities for 'design conscious' consumers in this country. Many of his methods were used

31 James Galt, a well-established supplier of educational toys through mail order, opened their first shop in Great Marborough Street in 1961.

earlier in the Sixties by Galt Toys, for example. Conran's particular contribution was to aim his goods at young, fashion-conscious, middle-class men and women in their twenties and thirties. When the London shop first opened, the shop assistants were given Sassoon haircuts and Quant outfits in a deliberate attempt to suggest that the shop was part of 'Swinging London': a fashionable place to go.

Although Conran had worked as a textile and furniture designer before moving to retailing, it was as a businessman rather than as a designer that he can be said to have been truly innovative. During the early Sixties, Conran found that the furniture he designed for the domestic market was selling very slowly from most existing retail outlets. The problem, as he saw it, stemmed from the fact that most furniture retailers were trying to be all things to all people, to show a 'general' range of furniture that would attract 'people in general'. Habitat, on the other

32 The use of natural materials and an almost total absence of packaging created a sophisticated anti-'hard-sell' approach which was designed to appeal to a certain sort of caring parent. Each design element combined to create a relaxed atmosphere as far from traditional toy selling as can be imagined.

hand, from the outset sold both furniture and household accessories that presented the customer with a 'ready made' style to take home. Items such as glass and tableware not only fleshed out that style, but also drew people into the shop without making them feel they had to make a major purchase; this was vital since most people buy large items of furniture infrequently.

The elements of Conran's 'ready made' style were mostly imported from other parts of Europe. The influence of France was evident not only in the types of cookware sold, but also in such display techniques as standing small items, like mugs or saucepans, in huge piles on the floor, as though in a warehouse. Conran liked the air both of utility and accessibility this method gave to the goods, whilst his buyer convinced him of its sales potential. The buyer had noticed that any customer taken into a stockroom would almost inevitably buy something: 'It's compelling, that warehouse atmosphere'[10]. Such displays also meant that there

33 It was Ken Garland's decision to link the names of James Galt's company at all times with the word 'toys'. By 1969 Garland had sufficient confidence in customer's familiarity with the idea to play games with the letters on the front cover of that year's catalogue.

34 Ken Garland and Associates acted as design consultants for James Galt and Company from 1961 to 1981. They were responsible for translating the ideas of honesty and simplicity suggested by the interior of the Great Marlborough Street shop, and by the construction of the toys themselves, into an overall graphic style for the company. The illustration shows the 1962/3 catalogue cover.

never mind; we guess you'll know it's Galt Toys

35   The rationalisation of shopping into a single building is, in objective terms, such an improvement on high street shopping, that it is necessary to balance the critic's talk of dull conformity with the requirements of the consumer who put access, safety and comfort higher than aesthetic considerations.

was initially no need for a stockroom, since all the stock was on view, on the shop floor. The goods themselves created the shopping environment.

MAIL ORDER

In spite of the influence of 'good design' shop interiors such as Habitat and the popularity of the boutique, the new face of shopping in Britain was, for better or worse, represented by schemes such as Shopping City, Runcorn, the numerous Arndale centres, and the countless shopping precincts that sprang up during the decade. These centres were, on the whole, highly profitable, but their success was surprisingly less spectacular than that enjoyed by the rise of mail order, which of all forms of retailing in the Sixties grew at the fastest rate. With its roots firmly in early twentieth-century working class culture, the extraordinary growth of the mail order companies was inextricably linked to a reaction to the rise of

36 'Shopping City' planned for Runcorn New Town in the late Sixties contained 500,000 square feet of shopping space, parking for 2400 cars as well as access for buses. The use of white tiles and picturesque grouping of the service towers created a futuristic vision of shopping: clean, dry and safe.

impersonalised shopping.

The system, by which a catalogue is held by an agent, is unique to Britain. The agent, usually a housewife, worked on a 10 percent commission, and it was her job to build up a network of customers who chose from the catalogue and ordered through her. As a form of credit buying, mail order was extremely advantageous; payment was spread over twenty or thirty-eight weeks and with no interest to pay. The weekly instalments for a Hotpoint Iced Diamond fridge, for instance, were £2 1s (£2.05) a week, in 1966. The attraction of mail order was not limited to favourable credit and the convenience of choosing goods in your own home; it also flourished on the sense of trust that dealing with a member of your own community brought. The companies prided themselves on their money-back guarantee, and on their concern for 'the neglected customer'. The combination of

the young trend

37 'The Young Trend' from Grattan's Mail Order Catalogue, Summer 1966.

a friendly agent and the knowledge that poor goods and bad service would have adverse effects on sales throughout the network, guaranteed a degree of 'consumer protection', rarely available in store shopping.

ADVERTISING AND SELLING: THE POSTER

From the late 1950s American advertising agencies began spreading to Europe, bringing with them techniques such as motivation and market research, as well as new working methods which involved the collective efforts of many people such as art directors, 'ideas men', writers and businessmen. Not surprisingly, this development upset many British poster artists who were accustomed to having the freedom both to conceive the design for a poster and to execute the image virtually unaided. For a while, many British poster artists saw themselves as operating in direct competition with newer American-style agencies. In turn, the agencies themselves were often reluctant to use the work of poster artists,

38　'Beanz Meanz Heinz' poster.

especially as the spell of photography increasingly took hold.

In 1964 a *Times* correspondent wrote that 'Photography is used in too many English advertisements today. Graphic design and the art of the poster . ... seem to have entirely disappeared from billboards in favour of enlarged photos'.[11] The tussle between the relative merits of photographic and hand drawn material affected many areas of graphic design during the Sixties, although it was perhaps most evident in advertising. The quarrel was clearly accentuated by the fact that many opponents of the growing use of photography, such as the *Times* correspondent, associated the trend with the 'spectre of Americanisation' which appeared to conservative cultural critics to haunt large areas of British life.[12]

By the end of the Sixties, *Design* magazine noted that many advertisers were increasingly able to entrust the entire message of an advertising poster to a photograph, which needed neither hand drawn illustration nor supporting text to make that message clear (apart from the name of the manufacturer of the goods being promoted).[13] As the tendency grew to advertise goods by associating them with certain ideas (particularly money or sex) rather than by emphasising the intrinsic qualities of the goods, so too did the apparent power of photography to present those ideas in glorious detail. The series of petrol adverts, 'Ride Regent – the lively one', were some of the most blatant and offensive attempts to sell a completely unrelated item through association with women's bodies, presented photographically.

Nonetheless, the latter years of the Sixties did see a tremendous resurgence of the popularity of hand drawn illustration, although not perhaps in the form the *Times* correspondent might have wished. From 1966/7 onwards, mainly under the influence of Californian poster artists, a particular kind of hand-drawn illustration grew in importance, based on swirling forms and astoundingly bright colours, bolstered by the happy plagiarising of all manner of earlier graphic styles. Its use in advertising was, however, mainly restricted to the promotion of goods for the youth market such as records, concerts or fashionable clothes.

39   In 1967 the Salvation Army
employed a leading advertising
agency, the KMP Partnership, to
conduct its campaign to raise £1
million. They used the work of leading
photographers for a series of posters
with the slogan 'For God's sake care,
give us a pound'. The images and
graphics were totally against the grain
of glossy advertising and 'Swinging
London' euphoria. The campaign
showed the way highly sophisticated
image-making could be used for non-
commercial purposes.

ADVERTISING AND SELLING: HOUSE STYLES

The Sixties saw a striking increase in the use of a particular kind of marketing and advertising: that of 'brand style' and 'corporate identity' projects. Both types of work involve the creation of a coherent graphic scheme through which a particular 'image' or style can be promoted. Brand images are usually applied to all manifestations of a particular brand of goods, such as packaging, advertising and shop displays, and are designed to appeal primarily to the consumer. Corporate images are usually designed for use on a wide range of objects associated with a particular company, such as stationery and buildings. The audience for this type of imagery can include people from both inside and outside the company, such as employees and investors as well as customers. Both types of scheme, however, involve a particular kind of selling: selling an image, or an idea.

One of the schemes most admired by the design establishment during the Sixties, was design company Wolff Olins' work for the British Oxygen Company. The early Sixties was a time of rapid expansion for BOC, and the company's management wanted to change their reputation from that of a rather conservative, UK based company, to one of a dynamic corporation of international importance. In 1966 Wolff Olins were called in to help. They devised a comprehensive scheme which was flexible enough to be applied to large vehicles as well as letter heads or site signs.

The functions of the style were various. Firstly, through variations of colour, it provided a means of uniting the wide range of BOC's subsidiary companies together, making clear their relationship both to each other and to the parent company. In this way the success of one part of the group could be reflected onto other parts through a shared visual identity. Secondly, the adaptability of the scheme meant that it could be applied to almost any object, and thus that almost any object could be turned into an advertisement for the company. Thirdly, Wolff Olins had carefully controlled the components of that style so that a particular set of ideas about the company were advertised (strength, a hint of aggressiveness), through a visual image that actively demanded attention.

Wolff Olins' work for Bowyers involved a slightly different set of concerns. Here their brief was to provide an image for a product rather than for a company. The appeal was therefore to be made primarily to the consumer, with part of the problem being to differentiate Bowyers' meat products from those of a company more familiar to consumers: Walls. Since the company thought that this could not be done by dramatically changing either the taste or the price of Bowyer's products, changing their visual appearance was one solution. The aim of the graphic scheme devised by Wolff Olins was partly to make the company seem older and more traditional than it was, and partly to capitalise on the fact that Bowyers were based in Wiltshire, an opportunity to use the rustic associations of the country to the full.

Wolff Olins' work for Bowyers was typical of much design work in the Sixties in that the design input, the image that was created, was the only way of distinguishing one product from another. With the advent of market and motivation research, each brand tended to become like the rest as each company's marketing team, frightened of losing out to its competitors, tended to come up with a similar identikit view of what the consumer wanted. Bread,

40 Aubrey Beardsley's work inspired many British poster artists during the Sixties, though few resorted to the wholesale plagiarism shown in this advertising poster for Elliott's boots. Surprisingly, the drapery on Beardsley's figures was re-arranged, and feathers added, to cover the breasts and pubic hair of some of the female figures. Customers could buy copies of this poster for 5s and display the shoe shop's advertising in their own homes.

washing powder and beer are good examples of staple goods which were produced by larger and larger companies, with the product being the lowest common denominator of the consumers' expectations. When this happens, as the advertising executive, David Ogilvy, suggested, 'the less part reason plays' in the customer's choice and the greater the importance of the marketer, advertiser and the designer. The reaction in the early Seventies to tasteless bread and gassy beer was led by a new breed of consumer groups such as the Campaign for Real Ale, who were able to force some manufacturers into re-thinking their claims that they were 'only giving the public what it wanted'.

Notes

1. Arthur Marwick, *British Society Since 1945*, Harmondsworth, 1982, p 116
2. David Gosling and Barry Maitland, *Design and Planning of Retail Systems*, London, 1976
3. Russell Miller, 'A Century of Sainsbury's, *Design*, no. 243, 1969
4. Elizabeth Ewing, *History of 20th Century Fashion*, 2nd ed, London 1975, p 186
5. Ken and Kate Baynes, 'Behind the Scene', *Design*, no.212, 1966, p 26
6. Mary Quant, *Quant by Quant*, London 1966, p 45
7. Barbara Hulanicki, *From A to Biba*, London 1983, p 99
8. Quoted in Francis Wheen, *The Sixties*, London 1982, p 170
9. Ibid, p 170
10. Barty Phillips, *Conran and the Habitat Story*, London 1984, p 27
11. Letter by Ashley Havinden, quoted in Alain Weill, *The Poster*, London 1985, p 315
12. See Dick Hebdige, 'Towards a Cartography of Taste 1935-1962' in *Popular Culture Past and Present*, London 1982, pp 194-218
13. Russell Miller, 'Success and Failure of British Posters' *Design*, no.245 May 1969, p 41

41 It was not only magazines which promoted the ideals of a complete interior. Show houses were also influential. This example from Runcorn New Town shows the rational, clean world of consumer goods and well designed not ostentatious accessories, which characterised the New Town idea.

42 Robin Day's 'Polyprop' stacking chair for Hille had a profound effect on British furniture design. It made use of recent innovations in technology, and its commercial success made manufacturers think seriously about making genuinely cheap mass-produced furniture.

DESIGN FOR LIVING

'It will be a great day when furniture and cutlery designs
(to name but two)
swing like the Supremes'[1]

The period from 1945-65 was one of enormous expansion in the furniture industry and in furniture retailing. The increased affluence of the average British family, and the ready availability of hire purchase schemes, meant that more people than ever were able to purchase new furniture. The media played an important role in promoting an awareness of design in the home. Apart from magazines like *Ideal Home* and the colour supplements, which were aimed at a predominantly middle-class market, the popular women's magazines such as *Woman* and *Woman's Own* also increased the amount of space given over to articles on home furnishing and Do-It-Yourself.

The same period also saw some of the most exciting advances made in the development of furniture for the mass market. New materials and manufacturing techniques developed during the war opened up a whole new range of possibilities for modern furniture. Advances in the manufacture of plywood and in the use of light metal alloys both had a knock-on effect for the furniture industry, but it was the development of plastics technology which effected the most profound changes in design for living.

Ideas for the innovative use of plastics in furniture design had been in common currency since the 1940s, when Charles Eames and others had developed prototypes for possible new forms. However, the large numbers of new synthetics which appeared in the Fifties and Sixties forced designers and manufacturers to look afresh at the application of plastics to domestic furniture. New materials exploited in the Sixties included resilient but flexible plastics for the moulding of seat shells, tables and other basically rigid items, and polyurethane foams which rapidly replaced sprung upholstery and foam rubber. The most consistently inventive designs using the new synthetic materials came from Italy, but a notable British success was the polypropylene stacking chair designed by Robin Day and first manufactured by Hille in 1963. A commercially significant feature of the new synthetics was that they could be moulded on a production line at high speed, and in the 'Polyprop' chair Hille produced a really low-cost mass production chair. It has been widely imitated and is still in production today.

The commercial success of the 'Polyprop', and other furniture designs using synthetics, underlines the importance of the contract sector — universities,

69

43 An oak stacking chair designed in 1960 by Professor R.D. Russell, one of 2000 made for Coventry Cathedral, consacrated in 1962. A number of different versions of wooden stacking and/or linking chairs were developed during the Sixties for conference halls or churches. The Gordon Russell chair is still in production.

44　The first domestic product to be made from bagasse, the waste product from sugar cane, Hille & Co's 'Kompas 1' occasional table was representative of attempts to introduce modern materials and mass-production methods into the furniture industry. The heat resistant finish and lipped top designed to prevent minor spills, made it particularly suitable for catering use.

business organisations, hotels etc — where evidence of new materials and techniques was more likely to be found than in the ordinary domestic interior. Whilst this undoubtedly reflects the innate conservatism of the domestic furniture market in Britain, traditional notions of comfort do tend to favour natural materials over synthetics. Symbolically important, in this respect, was the outfitting of the QE2, the new Cunard transatlantic liner launched in 1969, with interiors that served as a showpiece of contemporary British design.

Related to the taste for the impermanent in the Sixties, and a response, perhaps, to a need for design appropriate to urban living was the popularity of knock-down furniture and multi-functional pieces suitable to flexible modes of arrangement. It was found increasingly desirable for furniture to collapse, stack, fold or adapt itself to a variety of uses. By the mid-Sixties 'modular' was the word on everyone's lips, applied to bedroom, living-room and kitchen furniture, including room dividers. 'Why "Modular"?' asked one of the articles in the 1966 *Daily Mail Book of Furnishing, Decorating and Kitchen Plans,* and gave as the two main advantages of modular furniture the maximising of floor space and a heightened degree of flexibility.

45 The QE2 Restaurant chair designed by Robert Heritage for Race Furniture was the result of one of the most complex development programmes ever undertaken by a British chair manufacturer. It was made in brown for the Columbia Restaurant and in white for the Britannia.

46 William Plunkett's 'Coulsden' coffee table sold well both in the domestic and contract markets; several were made for use on the QE2. Its simplicity of structure was characteristic of much of the designer's work.

47 Nicholas Frewing's 'Flexible' easy chair for Race Furniture is a good example of the Sixties' vogue for 'knock-down' furniture. Ingeniously designed for home assembly, it also made storage and distribution easy for the manufacturer.

The former was thought to be particularly relevant to kitchen design, and the 'fitted' kitchen designed around standard units which are organised to take account of work-flow has, in the past twenty years, become a standard fixture in new houses and a selling point in older houses when a conversion has taken place. The chipboard carcases, which made up the various components of 'fitted' furniture, could be sold in a flat state for the consumer to assemble at home and, increasingly, many manufacturers sold their furniture in this way, thereby reducing the costs of warehousing, display and transport. This trend has continued to gain momentum since. The popularity of built-in storage space also meant that many traditional forms of cabinet furniture such as sideboards and

Wrighton
International

metric range
of
kitchen furniture

F Wrighton
+ Sons Ltd

48   By 1968 the British Standards Institute had begun its programme of changing from British Imperial Measure to the metric system in the construction industry. Wrighton's 'International' range of fitted kitchen furniture, which won a CoID award that year, was one of the first systems to be based on a 10cm module. The design was made more streamlined by replacing the usual line of top drawers with drawer units in vertical sections.

dressing-tables became outmoded, although the nostalgia boom of the late Sixties and Seventies brought them back into fashion amongst young consumers.

The 1966 Daily Mail book's second criterion for the success of modular furniture was flexibility, and it was this quality which was emphasised in the marketing of Max Clendinning's 'Maxima' range, which began to be manufactured by Race Furniture the same year. The range was based on sheets cut out of plywood and sprayed with paint in bold, bright colours. They could be used for chairs, tables or wall-hanging units by simply bolting them together in different configurations. The Daily Telegraph found the basic design 'ingeniously worked out' and providing 'endless opportunities for different combinations,' but had to admit that 'most people never get around to it and the chief advantage of all this versatility is for the manufacturer'.[2] Furthermore, although the concept and the bright colours suggested that the 'Maxima' range was aimed at the new youth market, the price (£49 10s for a large armchair and £37 for a dining chair) put it beyond the pocket of most people.

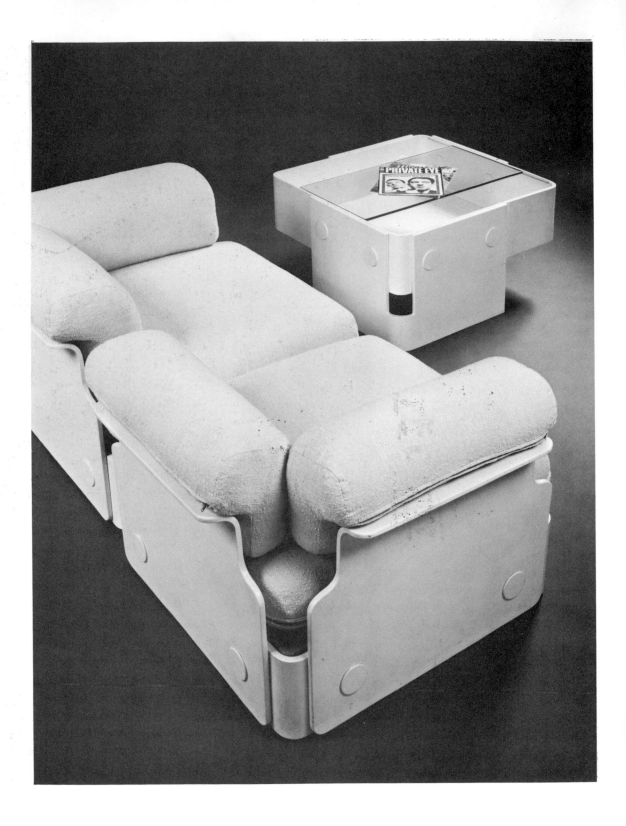

49 The 'Maxima' range by Max Clendinning for Race Furniture, first manufactured in 1966, epitomised the same youthful spirit as the futuristic fashions of that year.

50 Peter Murdoch's child's chair made of laminated paperboard was ingeniously constructed from a single piece for easy home assembly.

Race Furniture was one of a number of British manufacturers which attempted to exploit the 'Pop' market during the mid- to late-Sixties. Another was Hull Traders, a company best known for their furnishing textiles printed with abstract designs that were as bold in scale as they were in colour. Their 'Tom-o-tom' range of furniture designed by Bernard Holdaway also went into production in 1966. Made of compressed paper tubes and chipboard it was characterised, like most Pop furniture, by its bright, painted surfaces and by a lack of concern for durability. The ultimate manifestation of expendability in interior design, however, was paper furniture and inflatable furniture. A paper chair was first developed in Britain in 1964 by Peter Murdoch but was not marketed here until 1968. An inflatable chair, the 'Blow', was pioneered in Italy but versions were soon put on the market by British manufacturers.

Although the gap between Pop and the mass market may have narrowed a

51   Although the majority of the most exciting glassware designs came from Scandinavia during the Sixties, there were exceptions, such as these examples from a range of cut crystal glassware designed in 1963 by David Queensberry and made by Webb Corbett. The range won its designer the Duke of Edinburgh's Prize for Elegant Design in 1964.

52   A set of sherry glasses designed in the early Sixties by Ronald Stennett-Willson for Lemington Glass.

53   'Random' a bowl from David Queensberry's award-winning range. The glass was cut by hand, with the vertical lines crossed by random horizontal cuts to give a 'contemporary' air to a traditional, craft-based skill.

little in Britain during the Sixties, taste in furniture remained conservative rather than innovative. Many still preferred to live with reproduction furniture or second-hand pieces rather than commit themselves wholeheartedly to the new, and Fifties 'contemporary' styling still had its adherents. Also, there were whole sections of design-conscious people who hardly owned anything manufactured in Britain. Their furniture was Italian or Scandinavian, their glass Swedish, their appliances German.

All of the major stylistic shifts of the Sixties had their impact on furniture and

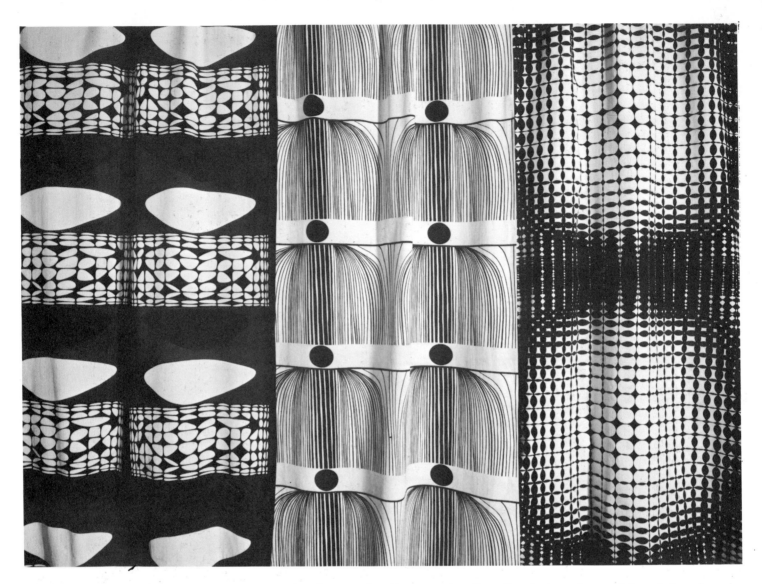

54　Wallpaper and textile designs influenced by Op Art. From left to right: 'Kernoo' by Victor Vasarely, 1963, manufactured by Edinburgh Weavers; 'Impact' by Evelyn Brooks, 1966, and 'Caprice' by Barbara Brown, 1964, both by Heal Fabrics.

55　'Telemachus', a wallpaper designed by Eddie Squires, for Sanderson's 1968 Palladio 8 collection.

interior design. Op Art was briefly influential in the middle of the decade, particularly on textile and wallpaper design. The mood of scientific adventure, which culminated in the first American moon landing in 1969, inspired a number of 'Space Age' furniture styles, but more prevalent were materials and colours associated with space travel, tubular steel and shiny white and silver. These features were also associated with a late Sixties revival of 1930s modernism.

Indeed, stylistic revivals represent one of the most significant developments of the later years of the decade. This nostalgia for the past, which was in marked contrast to the excitement about the future so evident in Sixties styling up to about 1967, was reinforced by the economic recession which was already under way by the early Seventies. Nostalgia is usually associated with conservatism, and so it is odd that it should have been appropriated by youth at this particular juncture.

56 A set of white polystyrene disposable cutlery designed by David Mellor for Cross Paperware in 1969. The designer's aim was to make the most of the strength of the material to produce usable cutlery which was cheap enough to be thrown away after use. It was originally intended for mass catering, but has since become popular with domestic users who, ironically, tend to wash and re-use it.

57 Cutlery commissioned from David Mellor in 1965 by the Ministry of Public Buildings and Works for use in government canteens, H.M. prisons and on British Rail. The design, 'Thrift' had five pieces rather than the customary eleven, whilst features such as the spoon's shallow bowls and the absence of a division between the handle and the blade of the knife, kept the number of production operations in manufacture to a minimum.

58 Trained as a silversmith, Robert Welch became interested in stainless steel during the late Fifties, and began designing items for mass production. As design consultant to Old Hall, he persuaded the company to drop the bright mirrored surface of their products in favour of a satin finish. These coffee pots, designed in the late Fifties sold well throughout the Sixties.

Barbara Hulanicki of Biba, stating her own preferences in interior decoration in 1966, explained: 'I love old things. Modern things are so cold'.[3] It should be noted, however, that the admiration for earlier styles was not accompanied, in the Sixties, by any longing to see the actual conditions of those times re-established.

Art Nouveau styles were the first to enjoy a popular revival. This was followed, before long, by a full-scale Victorian revival, particularly amongst young consumers who, throughout the decade, were busily gentrifying the working-class areas of Britain's major cities. When making its predictions for the Sixties, *Punch*, intending to make a joke, included the suggestion that the middle-classes would move to Islington; by 1970 it had become a fact.[4] Original Victorian and Edwardian furniture was bought at junk shops, and the wallpaper manufacturers,

59 'Arabesque', a high-fired earthenware coffee set, manufactured by Denby pottery in the early 1960s.

Sanderson's and Cole's, began to re-issue patterns by designers such as William Morris and CFA Voysey. The textile and wallpaper industries also issued many adaptations of Art Nouveau patterns carried out in the vivid colours of the late Sixties which came to be called 'psychedelic'. Psychedelia was the decorative art style of the hippy culture, which was also responsible for the popularising of a sort of obscure exoticism in interior design; its most common feature was the rejection of traditional seating in favour of littered cushions. Giant cushions, filled with polystyrene granules, were an inexpensive and popular item which found their way into many young people's homes in the late Sixties and Seventies as a substitute for chairs and sofas.

Items representative of most of these styles could be found in the eclectic mix

60 'Sedge', a bold design for a printed textile by Robert Dodd in 1962, manufactured by Edinburgh Weavers. The fairly realistic representation of plant forms is in marked contrast to the huge abstract patterns which were popular in the mid-Sixties.

61 'Sixty-three', an award-winning furnishing textile designed in 1963 by Shirley Craven. Craven was design consultant for Hull Traders, a firm with a reputation in the Sixties for adventurous design and bold colouring. The large scale of the repeat and the coherence of the design, whether flat or draped, endeared her work to architects.

which made Habitat such a successful business enterprise. Revivals of Victorian and Edwardian bentwood furniture were shown alongside sturdy stripped pine dining tables and benches, neo-Bauhaus tubular steel furniture along with flatweave rugs imported from the East. It is hardly surprising that, amongst the youthful middle-class, where design awareness had increased so dramatically in the Sixties, the Habitat look proved the most pervasive of the decade.

Perhaps more than in any other consumer item, except fashion, the style of furniture is of fundamental importance to its purchaser. In 1967, in an article entitled 'How will furniture develop?', David Pye wrote: 'We choose furniture, after all, just as we choose clothes, whether men's or women's, whether fashionable or not. We choose it primarily not for what it does but for what it says. We expect it to be useful but we want it, above all, to say something about ourselves.'[5]

Notes

1. Michael Wolff quoted in Penny Sparke, *Furniture*, London 1986, p 86
2. *The Daily Telegraph*, 1966
3. 'Take A Look At This New Face. It Belongs to 1966', *Daily Telegraph*, 27 October 1966.
4. Quoted in Francis Wheen, *The Sixties*, London 1982, p.170
5. David Pye, 'How will furniture develop?' *Country Life*, 23 March 1967

62 Candleholder in stainless steel with teak feet, designed in the late Fifties by Robert Welch for Old Hall Tableware.

63 An aerial view of Hulme, Manchester, 1965, showing the old street patterns before they were finally lost under the new estates. The sight of endless rows of back to back housing, at high density levels, was for many planners an unacceptable Victorian legacy unsuited to modern life.

64 An aerial view of Manchester, 1960.

THEMES IN PUBLIC HOUSING AND PLANNING

INTRODUCTION

The challenge for the decade as defined by the Royal Institute of British Architects at its annual conference held in Manchester in 1960, was nothing less than 'Rebuilding our Cities'. Manchester was an apt choice of location for the conference as its problems were typical of the great Victorian industrial cities.[1] The centre was dirty, overrun with cars, a patchwork of vacant warehouses and bomb sites surrounded by thousands of slums, many of which were located next to filthy factories and little better than those condemned a hundred years earlier by Engels. By 1960 giant strides had been made in rebuilding bomb-ravaged Plymouth and Coventry, and the first generation of new towns such as Harlow was taking shape but, as yet, little co-ordinated progress had been made with the problems of cities like Manchester. The programme of reconstruction that was finally unleashed in the Sixties had seen no parallel since the industrial revolution itself, and represented a commitment of capital and labour which marks it as one of the great collective efforts of the decade.

Ten years later a remarkable disillusionment had set in: slums had been replaced by 'sink estates'; better vehicle access had been achieved, but at the cost of urban motorways cutting ugly swathes through residential areas, and the rationalisation of land use into separate zones, intended to keep industry away from homes, had killed off much of the variety and vitality of city life. The environment may have been cleaner, but even this served to underline the point that much that was lost had been dirty rather than obsolete.

65 Manchester in 1969. In the course of ten years a number of office blocks had sprung up, including the Piccadilly Plaza development (top left) which in 1960 had been a bomb site used as a car park. Note also the cleaned Town Hall in the centre.

A sense of disillusionment continues to dominate popular opinion today. The architectural and planning professions are so fatally discredited that it is extraordinarily difficult to look beyond recent pictures of riots set against a backcloth of the new estates, to a period when modern architecture was widely expected to provide millions of people with better living conditions. To try and understand the heady idealism of the early Sixties is not to excuse an embattled profession for serious mistakes, but is rather an attempt to see how the newly built environment was the product of a broad range of social and political forces. To understand why 'improvement' proved so unpopular, it will require a close look at consumers and their role, or lack of it, in the design process.

NEW UTOPIAS

The Alton estate at Roehampton, Richmond, was in 1960 the most talked about and visited scheme in Britain. Nikolaus Pevsner called it 'one of the masterpieces of post-war residential design'[2]. Photographed from the correct position, with its clean elegant lines juxtaposed with mature trees and generously grassed areas, Roehampton's picturesque qualities reminded many of Georgian urban landscape at its best. For a few years at least Roehampton seemed to be a new and perfect embodiment of the finest social aspirations of the welfare state.

To understand the association of the modern style and the benevolent provision of mass public housing, one needs to examine the impact of the

66 View of Alton East, Roehampton. The most prestigious and influential British example of Le Corbusier's 'City in the Park' concept.

visionary ideals of the French architect, Le Corbusier. His concept of a 'city in a park' was persuasive not because of its stylistic novelty, but because of its social message. In 1936 he wrote: 'The benefits of the New Architecture must not be confined to the homes of the few who enjoy the privilege of taste or money. They must be widely diffused so as to brighten the homes, and thus the being, of million upon millions of workers'.[3] Architects had hitherto rarely concerned themselves with public housing; when they did enter the public arena after the war, the degree of naivety with which they frequently behaved, is painful to note. Herbert Read epitomised their crudely deterministic thinking: 'The only sin is ugliness', he wrote 'and if we believed this with all our being, all other activities of the human spirit could be left to take care of themselves.'[4] What was not apparent in the early Sixties was the degree to which it was not necessarily the modern style itself that was wrong, so much as the dominant model of state paternalism, by which improvements are imposed in what amounts to an authoritarian manner. It was well known that many people preferred small houses or bungalows with a private garden, but because council tenants did not have the financial independence to exercise the consumer's privilege of free choice, housing was provided on the basis of the subordination of individual interest and preference, to an ideal of communal organisation that was convenient to those who did the providing.

Reaction took a while to set in. For the first generation material improvements were often compensation enough for the loss of social identity and familiar places lost through wholesale redevelopment. But expectations rose, the problems posed by children and adolescents grew, and serious design and structural problems became more apparent. Even the picturesque location of Roehampton could not save the estate from experiencing many of the problems faced by its much less carefully designed and generously provisioned imitators. Michael Fleetwood believed that far from providing good homes for all and democratising the structure of society, in the end 'all that the modern movement has done, is to change the appearance of inequality'.[5] It is the *form* of Le Corbusier's architecture, the raw concrete, the 'brutalist' treatment of forms, and not the splendid ideals, which have moulded the urban environment. As Lewis Mumford suggested, the monotony and sterility of the modern style 'has expressed the dominant forces of our age, the facts of bureaucratic control and mechanical organisation .... They do not represent, in architectural form, the variety that actually exists in a mixed human community.'[6]

'WE HAVE THE TECHNOLOGY?'

At the beginning of a decade which was to see a man walking on the moon, it must have seemed perfectly reasonable to expect that the combined efforts of government agencies, local authorities and building contractors, would be able to produce a prefabricated building system that would be considerably cheaper and quicker than traditional building techniques. The basic premises of industrialised building were articulated by Walter Gropius, one of the pioneers of the modern movement. He believed that 'it will be possible to rationalise buildings and mass produce them in factories by resolving their structure into a number of component parts. Like boxes of toy bricks, they will be assembled in various formal compositions.'[7] But with over 300 different systems on the market by the mid-Sixties it was becoming clear that the degree of standardisation required was not feasible and that systems could never compete successfully in economic terms. With the collapse of Ronan Point tower block in 1968, it had become apparent that industrialised building had not even produced dwellings

67 Thamesmead Phase One made use of the Balency building system, whereby an on-site factory produced the concrete components which were quickly assembled in situ. The bold modelling of the forms and the picturesque use of its waterside location, drew the sort of attention accorded to Roehampton.

68 The initial concept model for Thamesmead. An overspill town for London, it was planned to eventually accommodate 60,000 people. The model, which was in brightly coloured plastic, contrasts strikingly with the concrete facing of the system used in the development.

69 One of the 22-storey blocks of flats built using the SFI system on the Elgin estate, Westminster, finished in 1968. In spite of the elegant, clean, machine-like efficiency of the cladding this system suffered, like many others, from problems with leaks.

70 The SFI system was claimed as the world's first use of wall panels in glass fibre reinforced plastics for a block of flats. The system was developed by the GLC, and depended on the use of technology originally developed for ambulance construction.

which were safe and waterproof. The sense of living in 'little boxes' piled on top of each other was an inevitable consequence of systems building.

The only major advantage of industrialised building lay in its speed of construction, whereby the basic frame and cladding produced in the factory or on site could be simply lifted into place using the minimum of skilled labour. It is a measure of the perception of the need for speed in the construction process that the three main political parties based their housing estimates for the 1966 election on the premise of the fullest use of systems. No party could be seen to be dragging its feet when there were still an estimated 1,800,000 slums to be dealt with. By 1965 a quarter of the 400,000 buildings produced by the public and private sectors were systems built, and according to the government this would have to increase to forty percent if the target of 500,000 for the next year was to be met.[8] Government subsidies were such that local authorities were actually subsidised if they used the more expensive but quicker systems. The Parker Morris Report concluded that a flat in a 12 storey block cost 50 percent more than a two storey house of equivalent size.

The sting in the tail for the local authorities came with the introduction of the cost yardstick, by which maximum costs for each housing unit were imposed by central government, and at levels which forced compromises. The role of the architect in systems building was in any case minimal; often they did little more than adapt the system so that it conformed to building regulations. Part of the failure of the architectural profession was actually an inability to influence design in the face of political and economic pressures. One architect who was forced to cut costs to meet the government yardstick, chose to remove every other paving stone from the garden path; faced with a typical dilemma he resolved it in a way that seemed to effect the consumer in the least adverse way. More stringent economies, however, inevitably affected the quality of the building adversely: corners were cut in the construction process; and when the building was completed essential services and maintenance were not always carried out — all elements which were beyond the direct control of architect or planner.

HOUSES, HOMES AND THE CONSUMER

Because of the notoriety of some public housing, building statistics for the Sixties can come as something of a surprise. In 1966 local authorities built 142,000 dwellings, compared with 207,000 built by private developers:[9] in fact the percentage of owner-occupied property was growing faster than local authority rented accommodation. The rise in the total housing stock meant that the average number of people per household dropped from 3.23 to 2.8, what would normally be considered a healthy index of affluence.

Private housing in the Sixties is very much the forgotten alternative. With the notable exception of W Cowburn's article 'Housing in the Consumer Society',[10] there is no analysis of the contribution of 'popular housing'. Cowburn predicted that: 'once the starvation in housing is alleviated everyone will demand housing which is now the choice of owner occupiers', and went on to isolate those elements of the modern semi-detached house or bungalow which were particularly relevant to owners' requirements. He talks of 'the house as an object', a consumer product, and points out the links 'between the house to be

owned and the car, the refrigerator and the pet animal. They can all be easily embraced mentally, and fulfil the desire for a symbol of an ideal life'.[11] The essential distinction Cowburn makes is between architects who build houses, and people who make homes, either through their personalisation of the impersonal housing environment or by exercising choice within a competitive housing market, or both.

One of the few examples in the Sixties of direct consumer intervention in the planning and design process of public housing was Ralph Erskine's project at Byker, Newcastle.[12] Erskine set up his office in the middle of the redevelopment area and actively sought out the future tenants' views. The result may have been every bit as monumental as much of the typical housing of the time, after all it was intended to form a 'wall' of housing against an urban motorway, but individual choices were allowed to determine the overall appearance of the development. The result was a sort of rustic, stylistic plurality, which gave the whole a disarming human scale.

The other area of public housing which did manage to avoid some of the pitfalls of the period, was in the New Towns. Because of their prestige status, and because of special administrative arrangements by which central government money was channelled through semi-independent Development Corporations, standards were compromised less. The New Town movement was also fortunate in being based on a rather more humane model of paternalism: the Garden City rather than the City in the Park.

Runcorn is typical of the second generation of New Towns designated in the Sixties to cope with the overspill from city centres. Much of the housing is low rise, neither good nor bad; but one scheme, The Brow, opened in 1968, managed to challenge a number of planning orthodoxies.[13] In particular it broke away from the example of Radburn, in the USA, which dominated planning, with its insistence on the absolute separation of motorist and pedestrian. In theory this should have been an obvious improvement in terms of environment and safety, but in practice, it often meant that the pedestrian, usually a woman, frequently with a child, was forced to follow tortuous routes and climb steps to use overhead walkways, whilst the car roamed free. Echoing the conclusions of Cowburn, the architects of The Brow, sought to develop the cul-de-sac into a pattern in which the car was controlled within a reasonably high density development, and which at the same time satisfied the ideal of surveillance within a communal format which was strictly human in scale.

The neglect of the consumer in the housing equation is particularly disappointing in view of the enlightened approach taken by the Parker Morris Report entitled 'Homes for Today and Tomorrow', published in 1961. The central recommendation that the architect should first 'define what activities are likely to take place in it (the home), then to assess the furniture and equipment necessary ... and then to design round these needs', was surely a call to recognise the consumer's needs. The way events developed only reinforced the dichotomy of homes/housing into private/public ownership. The language of private developers' advertisements and consumer magazines, (Ideal Home, etc) underlined the notion of 'home' as ownership, whilst councils invariably talked about housing ('Housing Committee' etc). Given the sense of alienation felt by many people moved into accommodation of objectively higher standards, a truer definition of home might thus be 'belonging within', rather than 'belonging to'.[14]

71 The Brow estate in Runcorn New Town was one of the first developments to challenge the planning orthodoxy that pedestrians and cars must be separated. The use of traditional materials and the 'cul-de-sac' form shows the debt to 'popular housing', that is housing produced by builders for the private sector.

72 Oscar Newman in his book *The Defensible Space* identified the optimum conditions in which crime and vandalism are 'easy to commit and difficult to prevent: anonymity, lack of surveillance and the presence of alternative escape routes'.

73 The picturesque arrangement of forms along a dramatically receding avenue is typical of the predominant concern for appearance in planning in the Sixties. The view from inside is rather less interesting.

74 The access balcony and the shared, communal open space are no substitutes for the sense of belonging and the feeling of security, in both real and symbolic terms, that are guaranteed in terraced housing by traditional street patterns and private gardens.

75 As the example of the American
penthouse suggests, height alone is
not the problem. Poor services,
inadequate lifts and the misconceived
policy of putting large families from
the top of housing lists into flats, has
resulted in Britain in the general
equation of high rise and housing
failure.

76 Harold Wilson, on an official visit to Manchester in the mid-Sixties, is seen inspecting the model of the City Centre.

'REBUILDING OUR CITIES'

With the exception of London, which has always had the financial clout to undertake a fairly continuous renewal of its building stock, the major industrial cities had seen little redevelopment. By 1960 there were signs that the enormous property boom, mainly speculative office development, which had begun in London in the mid-Fifties after the removal of post-war building restrictions, was beginning to move north.[15] The fact that new developments had been held back for nearly a generation, together with the availability of ready capital for investment, created fertile conditions for a crop of ambitious entrepreneurs to reap spectacular benefits. Coupled with this, cities like Birmingham, Liverpool, and Manchester were setting up Planning Departments to co-ordinate and direct the transformation of the city environment. People's standards and expectations of city life were growing; what was good enough for the citizens of Harlow New Town ought to be good enough for the industrial north.

City Planning Departments could put together any number of advisory plans for the development of their city, but implementation required the working together of council and developer.[16] In theory the two sides both stood to gain; the developer often required the help of the council's compulsory purchase powers in order to consolidate ownership of a large site, and they always required planning permission. The council in turn needed an investor who could help to bring jobs and revenue to the centre through developments which could also assist with overall planning goals. In practice this relationship unfortunately

77 Development proposals such as the Arts Centre for Manchester suffered a variety of fates. Many Sixties planning proposals are only now coming to fruition, whilst others, as in this case, have realised via a series of ad hoc solutions using existing buildings.

tended to favour just one side. As long as there was another city competing for investment and jobs, the council felt itself in a weak bargaining position, when, or if, the developer decided that a few extra storeys, or the substitution of concrete for Portland stone was essential to maintain profit margins. Councils often managed to include a library, a row of shops or a cherished pedestrian scheme as part of an office development, but this did little to stave off violent public criticism when the corrupt practices of a few tarnished the council/developer relationship for good.

THE OBSOLETE CENTRE?

With the benefit of hindsight, the 'obsolete centre', as defined by Planning Departments, was not perhaps the clearcut, objective issue it had seemed in 1960. The rise of the conservation movement in the Sixties and our greater experience with the refurbishment of buildings, makes it difficult to think back to a situation when blanket demolition and rebuilding of whole areas seemed the only choice. But such must have been the contrast between the overwhelming filth which covered architectural masterpieces as well as humble warehouses, and the gleaming glass and aluminium of developers' tower blocks, that it is not entirely surprising that buildings which we now cherish (perhaps in their cleaned state), could have been regarded as expendable. When the full glory of Manchester Town Hall was liberated from the black mantle that had obscured the building for generations, it was both a symbol of Sixties idealism and desire for improvement at its best, and also a sad reflection on much that had been lost.

At the same time there was also a growing feeling that the rationalisation of a confused pattern of land use into distinct functional zones, had robbed the urban area of much of its variety and vitality. Rationalisation made economic sense: warehousing and industry benefited enormously from the greater accessibility of out-of-centre locations. Likewise there were benefits to the environment when industry was relocated away from housing, and slum clearance schemes also reduced the intolerable housing densities. But the consequences of often laudable schemes were not always foreseen and not always beneficial. Thus the concentration of the centre into essentially a business, shopping and entertainment core, not only continued, but speeded up the process of the decentralisation of housing. The better off were more mobile and able to afford expensive houses in the suburbs, and it was for them that the improved road system particularly catered. Those left behind in the inner city estates tended to include a large proportion of ethnic minorities and large families united by disadvantage. The centre itself, in the absence of residents, was left dead and unused outside office hours.

The new restricted view of the function of the city centre was demonstrably cleaner and safer for the user, but, in common with the reaction against modern housing and roads, was often unpopular. The old city was objectively deficient, but its familiarity, its more human scale, allowed for specialisation within the local area; it allowed the growth of what Nicholas Taylor called the 'Village in the City' concept. [17] An urban format which is based on the aggregate needs of individuals, like the Byker Wall, is not pretty, but it is a reflection of the fullness of human experience, in a way that the picturesque approach to planning, which puts the central emphasis on appearance and order, can never be.

What is at stake here, and what unites architecture and planning with the sort of debate carried on in design circles, is the issue of good taste. Just as the Council of Industrial Design asserted certain standards of good design based on rational design principles, so too did the architectural and planning professions, who failed to see that the dogmatic pursuit of grand universal solutions based on Modernist principles completely ignored the symbolic element of house or city. A PVC trouser suit evinces a similarly unfeeling indifference to the comfort of the wearer as the concrete tower block; both were designed as though they were only to be looked at. The tragedy of architecture is that you cannot just throw the

78 Improved access to the centre involved the building of roads which cut through residential areas. In this case the footbridge forms a gentle curve which means that a pedestrian starting from one end cannot see the person or persons approaching from the other.

79 Manchester Town Hall during its cleaning in 1966/7.

80 An early view of the model of the
city centre, Manchester, showing the
proposed inner city ringway. The plan
was dropped in the mid-Sixties on
environmental grounds. This was to
be the fate of many schemes
throughout the country, which, if they
had been fully implemented, would
have resulted in cities much closer to
the American example.

81 Improved access to the centre meant the need for more parking space. The Buchanan Report on *Traffic in Towns* concluded that if everybody who worked in the centre drove to work, the whole city would have to be reconstucted: an element of control was therefore necessary. The parking meter was first introduced in 1959.

82 The Runcorn New Town busway was one of the most successful attempts to provide public transport which did not have to compete with the car. The bus-only routes, serviced by a network of paths, connect the residential, industrial and shopping areas, and provide a frequent, cheap service.

83 An artist's impression of the Manchester Transit System which, like many radical public transport alternatives in the Sixties, did not get beyond the report stage. Car ownership doubled in the decade and the priority placed on catering for the car remained virtually unchallenged.

MANCHESTER RAPID TRANSIT SYSTEM

building away after a few months; people have to live on in the mistakes. The challenge that youth culture and Pop design posed to the established canons of 'good taste' never really stood a chance against the powerful and entrenched position of state paternalism, left and right, in the Sixties.

Notes

1. See the articles on Manchester produced to coincide with the conference: *The Architect and Building News,* 15 June, 1960, p 755 ff; *The Architect's Journal,* 16 June, 1960, p 891 ff

2. See Michael Fleetwood, 'Building revisited: Alton Estate, Roehampton', *The Architect's Journal,* March 30, 1977, pp 593-603

3. Lionel Esher, *A Broken Wave. The Rebuilding of England 1940-80,* London 1981, p 8

4. Op cit, Fleetwood, p 603

5. Ibid, p 603

6. Malcolm MacEwen, *Crisis in Architecture,* London 1974, p 17

7. Sutherland Lyall, *The State of British Architecture,* London, 1980, p 45

8. Anon, 'Supplement on Industrialised Building', *The Times,* March 21, 1966

9. See Butler and Sloman, *British Political Facts 1900-75,* London, 1977

10. *Architectural Review,* November, 1967, pp 398-400

11. Ibid, p 399

12. Op cit, Lyall, p 137

13. See Eddie Jenkins and Mike Jenks, 'Project Revist: Halton Brow, Runcorn', *Architectural Journal,* 21 March, 1979, pp 585-96

14. See Nicholas Taylor, 'The Failure of 'Housing', *Architectural Review,* November, 1967, pp 341-59

15. See Oliver Marriott, *The Property Boom,* London, 1967

16. See City of Manchester Planning Department, *City Centre Map 1967*

17. Nicholas Taylor, *The Village in the City,* London, 1973

THE SWINGING SIXTIES?

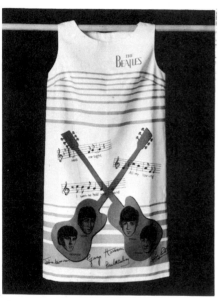

84 One of the many souvenirs produced in 1963-4 to exploit 'Beatlemania'. The souvenir trade was the most obvious of example of minimal design input and marketing being all-important.

FASHION

Between 1945 and 1960 the wages of British teenagers rose twice as fast as those of adults and, since unemployment in the early Sixties was around 1 percent, most young people enjoyed the benefits of this increase in spending power. Unburdened by the financial obligations of adults (rent, rates, heating bills etc.), a significant proportion of their money was spent on clothes. In 1967 the 15-19 age group, which had constituted a tiny fraction of the buying market in the mid-Fifties, accounted for almost 50 percent of all clothes bought.[1] Not surprisingly, this had a considerable influence on the sort of clothes which were fashionable and on the way in which fashion was presented in the media.

High fashion (the dress of the fashionable avant-garde) in Britain during the ten years from about 1963 until 1972 was characterised by lively inventive clothes which showed a total disregard for the conventional categories of day and evening, formal and casual, and for the notion of seasonal collections (Mary Quant designed twenty-eight collections a year at the beginning of her career). There was, moreover, a tendency towards increasingly frank displays of the body. Quite apart from the topless dresses and body painting which made good editorial copy but which were never part of mainstream fashion, the decade saw a variety of clothes with cut-out or see-through details. The garment, however, which was the ultimate in youthful assertion and daring was the mini-skirt. It has become, in many people's eyes, possibly the most memorable visual symbol of the Sixties and, for the first time in history, it brought women's thighs into focus as an area of erotic interest. The expression 'mini-skirt' began to be commonly used in 1965, although the hemline had been rising gradually for a year or two before that. It is, moreover, a comparative term since, in contrast to the highly abbreviated skirts of the end of the decade, those of the mid-Sixties now appear fairly modest. In spite of the fashion trade's repeated endeavours to introduce longer skirts from 1968, skirts settled above the knee or higher amongst all age groups until the early 1970s.

As skirts rose and legs were more on view, stockings became a fashion item in themselves and were made in bold colours or interesting textures. Tights first appeared in 1960 but were worn initially for reasons of warmth rather than fashion; they became a necessity as the mini-skirt rose to a level which made a

85 Rootstein's mannequins captured the movement and stance, make-up and hairstyles of the photographic models and 'dolly' girls who made up the London fashion scene. These three mannequins were based on Donyale Luna, an angular black model from Detroit, who was a great favourite with fashion photographers in 1966.

86 One of the most popular dresses of 1965 was made entirely of crochet, and many others had cut-out or see-through details. In response, a number of hosiery and underwear manufacturers introduced flesh-coloured body-stockings into their ranges. This dress, worn by Jean Shrimpton, and designed by John Bates for Jean Varon was selected as Bath Museum of Costume's 'Dress of the Year'

87. The Adel Rootstein Studio released its first collections in reponse to the need for mannequins that would relate to the clothes being produced by the new wave of young British designers. The 'Twiggy' collection was released in 1966.

88 Mini skirts as seen in the 1965 film, *The Knack,* directed by Richard Lester. By the end of the decade the word 'mini' would refer to a skirt at least seven inches shorter.

gap between stocking and skirt almost inevitable. It did, however, take some time for tights to take over from stockings in the hosiery market. In 1969 tights still accounted for only 160.9 million pairs out of a total of over 470 million pairs of hosiery whereas, today, they completely dominate the market.[2]

The quality and finish of much Sixties' boutique fashion left something to be desired. Biba clothes, in particular, were criticised as 'badly made', perhaps because they were cheap and run up so quickly. Yet it hardly mattered, since durability was not, on the whole, what the boutique clientele put high on its list of fashion requirements. Nor was comfort, it appears. Barbara Hulanicki wrote of the 'uncomfortable Biba smock that itched' and of 'long skinny sleeves ... so tight they hindered the circulation'.[3]

The new approach to manufacturing and selling young fashion had its effect on both couture at one end of the market and the chain stores at the other. The demise of the great French couture houses was already under way by the beginning of the Sixties, but the speed with which ideas could be copied and the dresses find their way into the shops forced a number of influential couturiers into ready-to-wear fashion. One such was Courrèges, whose much-acclaimed Spring 1964 space-age collection was widely plagiarised. Another was Yves St Laurent: within a matter of weeks dresses based on his 1965 Mondrian collection were in high street shops all over Britain.

The Sixties also saw the beginning of a breakdown in sexual differentiation through dress, leading to what later became known as 'unisex' fashions.

89 One of the attractions of clothes from Biba was their price; the suit shown on the left cost £7 7s in 1969, whilst a comparable suit designed by Zandra Rhodes sold for £16. Photographed for a Biba mail-order catalogue, 1969.

Although trousers had been worn by women for leisure activities since the 1920s the Sixties saw them accepted in the workplace and for more formal occasions. Felicity Green of the *Daily Mirror* gave this as her reason for selecting a trouser suit as the Bath Museum of Costume's 1967 *Dress of the Year*. Likewise, the Sixties also witnessed men's dress emerging from the sobriety which had largely characterised it since the end of the eighteenth century. There took place throughout the decade experiments with materials, colours, and patterns hitherto considered quite impossible in the male wardrobe, and under the influence of the hippies young (and sometimes not so young) men began to grow their hair long from about 1967. John Stephen, with his string of Carnaby Street shops, did for men's dress what Mary Quant had done for women's – acted as a catalyst for change. For a while the fear of being labelled effeminate held men back, so in 1962 John Stephen had a range of his clothes modelled by Billy Walker (Walker was, at the time, the great hope of British boxing, and so widely admired that not even pink denim could cast aspersions on his manhood).

A number of youth sub-cultures exerted an influence on fashion in the Sixties. Early in the decade the mods had been highly individual stylists in the true Beau Brummell tradition. As Carnaby Street changed from being the stamping ground of a rather precious minority to a world-famous tourist attraction, 'mod' became a generic term to describe young fashions in general. Via television programmes like *Ready Steady Go*, which first went on the air in 1964, and fashion magazines like *Honey*, mod styles in this broader sense were transmitted to teenagers in the provinces.

90 Diana Rigg as Emma Peel, wearing 'VIP', a wool trouser suit designed by John Bates for Jean Varon. The jacket had white PVC tabs and a PVC belt. The suit cost 30 ½ guineas.

In complete contrast, the hippies, who took their lead from American youth, pursued a policy tantamount to anti-fashion. Clothes were thrown together at random, their colours clashing wildly. It represented a deliberate challenge to the ideals of consumerism, which became even more pointed when 'flower power', in full bloom from 1966-7, was replaced by a deliberate scruffiness. The main source of hippy fashion was ethnic. From 1967, and into the early Seventies, garments and jewellery of Indian, Middle Eastern and South American origin

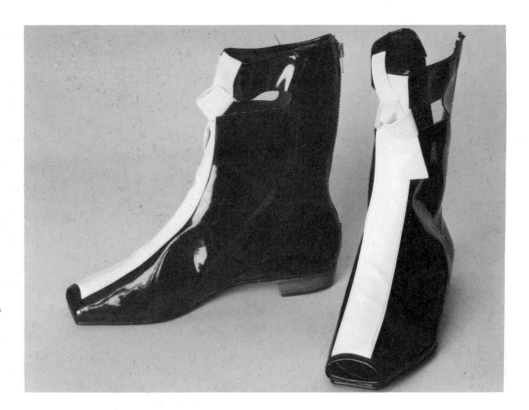

91 The calf-length, white leather boots which Courréges showed with most of the clothes in his 'space age' collections of 1964-5 were widely copied, usually in synthetics. These are 'Career Girl' boots in black and white PVC, sold by Lotus.

were adopted first by the hippies and then absorbed into the mainstream of fashion.

Ethnic styles in dress were part of the same taste which preferred floor cushions and Oriental rugs to more conventional seating and fitted carpet. Both reflected a sense of disillusionment and dissatisfaction with contemporary culture, felt by many young people from 1967-8, and who began to seek alternatives. It appears that, at times of social crisis, there is a tendency for some to look back, to a past perceived as being simpler and closer to nature than one's own, and to admire also, and for similar reasons, contemporary societies perceived as being more primitive. There are historical examples of this phenomenon (in the second half of the eighteenth century, for example) and, certainly, in the late Sixties, endless revivals of past styles went hand in hand with a pronounced taste for the exotic in design.

The expansion of the fashion industry in the post-war period has made it one of the most immediate and most sensitive recorders of changes in the social climate and of shifting tastes and influences. The mid-Sixties saw fashions inspired by new technology (PVC was used for the first time in fashionable clothing), by exploration into space, and by both Op and Pop Art. Similarly, as the nostalgia boom of the latter part of the decade began to make its mark on design in general and people began collecting the furniture, jewellery, ceramics and graphics of the Art Nouveau and Art Deco periods, the two years from 1967-8 saw a transition from futuristic to romantic fashions. In menswear, from the upmarket but highly fashionable Blades of Savile Row through to mass market

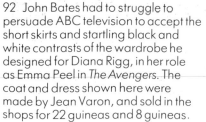

92 John Bates had to struggle to persuade ABC television to accept the short skirts and startling black and white contrasts of the wardrobe he designed for Diana Rigg, in her role as Emma Peel in *The Avengers*. The coat and dress shown here were made by Jean Varon, and sold in the shops for 22 guineas and 8 guineas.

C & A Modes, the Edwardian suit, high-collared and double-breasted, reigned supreme. In women's dress the influence of the 1930s and 1940s tended to prevail over the earlier period and, by the very end of the decade, the antique market for old clothes had opened up properly and the genuine article was worn alongside contemporary versions of it.

High fashion is, of course, never the whole story, and the sartorial upheavals of the Sixties were nothing like as dramatic as the media would have one believe. Away from Chelsea and Kensington, on the streets of Manchester and Leeds, the

93 For interior shots, fashion photographer John French used large white boards to reflect light onto the models, giving a softer effect than the harsh glare of direct lighting. Clothes and models benefited from the elimination of shadows, blemishes and wrinkles. Any remaining imperfections were removed by re-touching by hand. Models in PVC trouser suits photographed for the *Daily Mirror,* autumn, 1965.

94 The technical qualities of John French's photographs were specially adapted for reproduction in newsprint, enabling newspaper Art Editors to make greater use of photos rather than hand-drawn illustrations. Such sophisticated fashion images thus reached wider audiences during the Fifties and early Sixties. Photograph by John French of Jean Shrimpton modelling a Young Jaeger suit, c.1963.

95 High contrast photographs were used by the Vidal Sassoon salons to promote the ideal of a heavy, shiny head of hair cut to emphasise movement. This style, called an 'A' line bob, was introduced in 1966.

96 Vidal Sassoon used the word 'geometric' to describe hairstyles such as this cut, introduced in 1966, with sharp angular lines framing the face.

speed of diffusion of avant-garde styles in women's dress was greater by far than its counterpart in menswear. Carnaby Street as a design concept did make most men more fashion-conscious, and forced manufacturers to introduce more style and colour into their ranges for the younger customer but, for the majority of men, the newsworthy face of Sixties' fashion would always be too effete and flamboyant.

SELLING FASHION

The visual and verbal imagery through which ideas about women's fashions were developed in all branches of the media from the early to mid-Sixties, relied heavily on ideas associated with freedom and liberty. The pinafores introduced by Mary Quant were presented as freeing women from the necessity of constricting their waists to an exaggeratedly small size; the gradual shortening of skirt lengths from the late Fifties onwards seemed to emphasise freedom of movement; changes in underwear, with tight-fitting corsets being discarded in

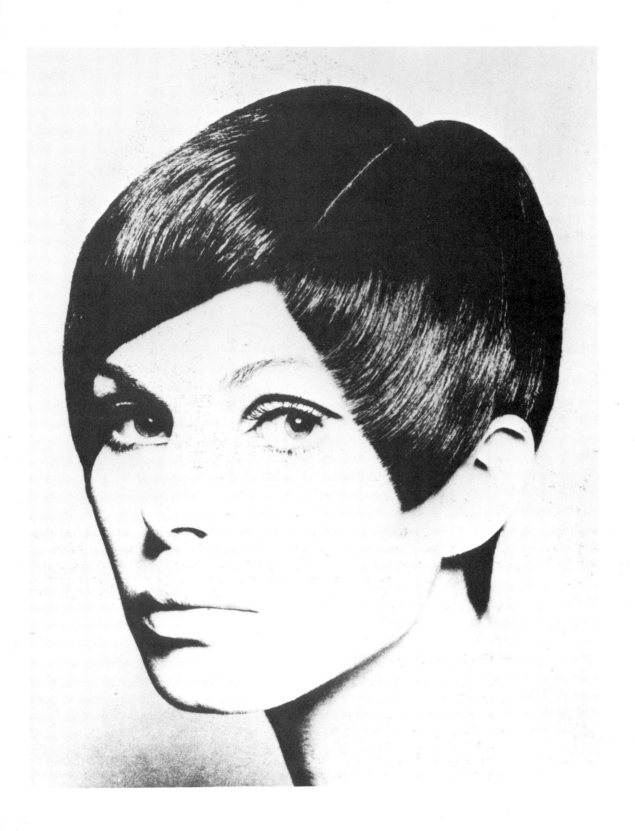

97 Twiggy's eyes being matched for colour and size at Madame Tussaud's during the preparation of a wax model. Twiggy's entry into the Pantheon of popular esteem followed swiftly on from her being voted 'The Face of '66'.

favour of smaller, looser garments, equally seemed to present women with the freedom to move and behave 'more naturally'. Such ideas were reinforced by fashion photographers, who moved away from the frozen poses of Fifties fashion shots towards images of women moving, sometimes even running or jumping. Likewise, Vidal Sassoon's haircuts were calculated to emphasise movement. Back-combing and hairspray were frowned upon, and replaced by an ideal of a heavy, shiny head of hair that moved freely and easily.

However, in spite of the way in which they were presented, these new ideas clearly did *not* liberate women from the repressive aspects of earlier fashions. All that happened was that the new fashion forms imposed a different, though equally powerful, kind of constraint upon those women encouraged to follow them.

Particularly noticeable was the changing ideal of a woman's body. During the late Fifties and throughout the Sixties, the ideal figure for a woman presented through the fashion media, became further and further removed from that of a

XI The first posters Michael English and Nigel Weymouth designed together were advertisements for rock concerts, such as these 'Coming Events' at the London club 'UFO'. The influence of Alphonse Mucha's poster designs is very clear.

121

XII During the Sixties men's ties became a colourful and highly-patterned dress accessory. The kipper-shaped tie, with a blade as wide as 5 or 6 inches, was produced in a range of flamboyant designs and bold colours, and was often worn with the most sober of business suits from around 1967.

XIII The fold-out circular 'tobacco tin' cover for the Small Faces' *Ogden's Nut Gone Flake* LP, 1969, was one of the more impractical designs to win a CoID award during the Sixties.

XIV Martin Sharp's cover for Cream's *Disraeli Gears*, Polydor, 1967, shows the striking impact made by the work of the Californian graphic designers, with their combinations of collage, swirling vegetative forms and day-glo colours.

XV The 4.2 litre E-type Jaguar. This particular model was a left-hand drive version, and was used as a show car on the Cunard liner, the *Queen Elizabeth*, on the Atlantic route.

XVI An alternative design submitted by Ann and David Gillespie for the 'British Technology' stamp issue, September 1966. The use of the Mini, E-Type Jaguar and the Moulton bicycle together underlined not only their export value but also their significant symbolic power to evoke all that was best in British industrial design.

XVII 'Salome' storage tins, table mats and coasters, with the 'Harriet' square tray, all designed by Ian Logan.

98 The alarming
potential consequences
of the cult of thinness
focussed around Twiggy
were well represented by
Cecil Beaton's
photographs for *Vogue*
in October, 1967. So
diminutive in size, the
woman is also
diminished in
consequence: Beaton
described Twiggy as 'a
sort of butterfly
person...a weightless
marshmallow.'

XVIII Centre Point was designed by R Seifert and Partners for the property developer
Harry Hyams, and was completed in 1965.

99 The distortion created by camera angles which increase the apparent size of the models' heads, coupled with eye make-up so heavy as to make the eyes appear to have enlarged, blackened sockets, introduces a particularly disturbing element into the marketing of a fashion ideal. This is compounded by the handcuffs worn here by the model on the right. From Biba's mail order catalogue for summer 1968; photography by Hans Feurer, model Stephanie Farrow.

100 The brief vogue for broderie anglaise, frills and pale pastel colours during 1967 surrounded women with ideals of innocence and purity based on the association of such colours and materials with babies layettes. Photograph by 'Just Jaeckin' for *Vogue,* May 1967.

fully developed, physically mature woman, towards that of a young, pre-pubescent girl whose breasts and hips had not yet filled out. With the *Daily Express*'s promotion of Twiggy as 'The Face of'66', the adulation of thinness was given fresh impetus, eventually reaching the alarmingly skeletal proportions promoted by the fashion photography for *Biba* mail order catalogues of 1968/9. Discussing this adulation of deprivation and deformity, Barbara Hulanicki writes, with no apparent irony, that girls who wore Biba clothes

'were the post-war babies who had been deprived of nourishing protein in childhood and grew up into beautiful skinny people. A designer's dream.'[4]

Almost inevitably, there developed alongside the increasing pressure on women to diet, a growing recognition of the perils of bulimia and anorexia nervosa (both varieties of eating disorder). These affected many women who tended to focus their emotional problems around the enormous difficulties they experienced in meeting an ideal of such exaggerated thinness.

The twin ideals of youth and slimness were of course closely related. At times it seemed as though there was no limit to the lengths to which fashion 'looks' would go to escape from the appearance of a mature female body, as fashions in women's dress appropriated the appearance not only of schoolgirls, but also of adolescent boys, or even babies. Quant's pinafore dresses and short white boots made obvious references to girls' school uniforms, whilst the fashion for 'skinny-ribbed' sweaters was described by Quant as resulting from her having 'one day ... pulled on an eight year old boy's sweater for fun'; she was 'enchanted with the result'.[5] At the same time, the appeal of the heavy eyeliner and false eyelashes which made women's eyes look unnaturally large was clearly related to the appeal of the proportions of babies' faces, both animal and human. Mary Quant describes the overall change thus:

'There was a time when every girl under twenty yearned to look like an experienced, sophisticated thirty ... all this is in reverse now ... suddenly every girl (aims) to look ... under the age of consent'.[6]

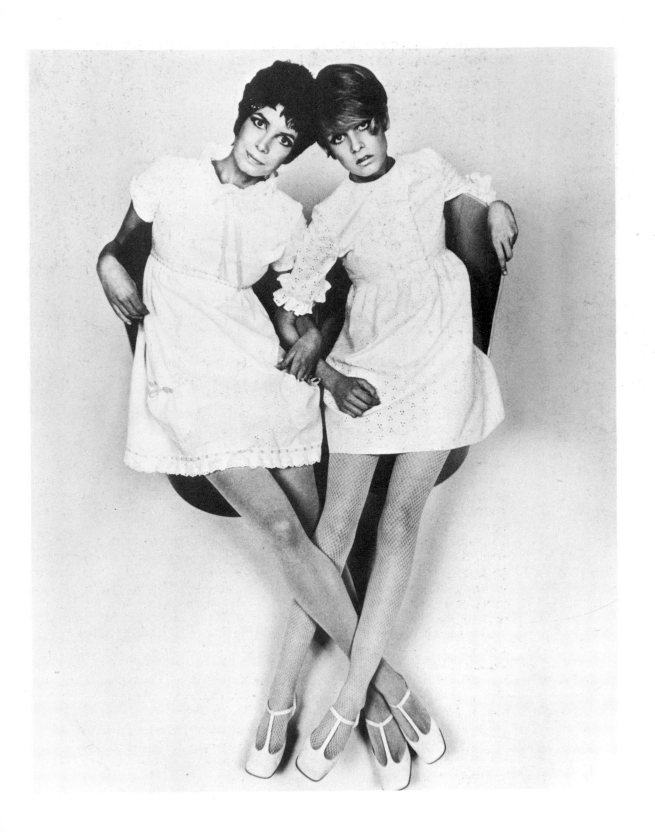

101, 102 The Sixties are remembered as ushering in the 'permissive society' and sowing the seeds of the feminist movement in this country, but sexual stereotypes retained a strong hold. Terence Stamp and Julie Christie in John Schlessinger's 1967 film *Far From the Madding Crowd*.

Hinted at here is the class-related basis of such a change, with the manners and behaviour of this younger fashion ideal being associated with women of a lower social class than the 'sophisticated society girl'[7] whom Brigid Keenan describes as having been the popular heroine of the mid-Fifties.

Alongside the visual imagery created by fashion photographers, there developed a mode of writing which operated by applying verbal imagery which would appear to 'naturalise' the extremes of distortion taken up by fashion promoters. The vegetable imagery applied to women's legs as it became fashionable for them to grow longer and longer now seems laughable; Barbara Hulanicki described the 'classic Biba dolly' as having 'long asparagus legs'[8], whilst *Vogue* magazine in 1968 introduced a new model, Penelope Tree, who had legs 'as long as sunflower stalks'.[9]

GRAPHICS FOR A YOUTH MARKET

Evidence that England was 'swinging' in the Sixties was found by contemporary journalists not only in the fashion industry but also in pop music. As far as design was concerned, the evidence was particularly striking in two areas connected

103 Michael Caine as Harry Palmer in *The Ipcress File,* 1965. The idea that Britain was becoming 'classless' during the Sixties was widespread. The success of people such as Michael Caine, despite the fact that his class origins were emphatically clear, was often cited in evidence. A 1971 government report, however, showed little change in the basis of such class divisions. The distribution of earnings remained much the same as in 1886; material hardship may have diminished, but *relative* deprivation persisted.

104 During the summer of 1965 the press became obsessed with a group of people supposedly at the heart of 'swinging' London. Encapsulated by David Bailey's *Box of Pin Ups,* 1965, their attraction centred around the glamour of sudden wealth, however obtained. When the Kray brothers were tried in 1969, the questionable nature of Bailey's presentation of them became unavoidably clear. *Private Eye* used Bailey's photo of the Kray's in March 1969.

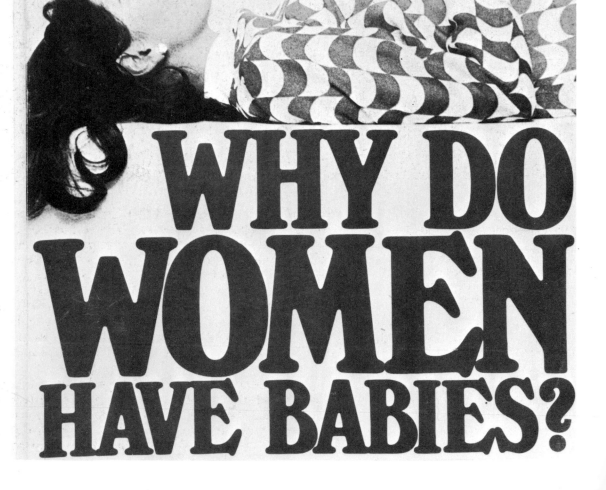

MAY 1967 THREE SHILLINGS

NOVA

STARTING
LEN DEIGHTON'S
NEW SPY BOOK.
ALSO DAVID FROST,
MOREAU BROPHY,
SHRIMPTON,PROOPS,
LADY CHICHESTER

WHY DO WOMEN HAVE BABIES?

105 *Queen* and *Nova* paraded the daring with which they tackled contemporary issues such as birth control by such startling conjunctions of photography and typography as this front cover of *Nova*, May 1967.

106 Double-page spread from *Nova*, November 1969. Innovation in design, layout, photography and typography introduced by colour magazines such as *Queen* and *Nova*, played a major part in propagating the myth of 'swinging' London, suggesting that Britain was rushing headlong into an era of unprecedented change and excitement.

with pop music: posters advertising concerts and records, and LP covers.

The growing adventurousness of LP covers for pop records was in fact largely a Sixties phenomenon. Although there was a market for rock 'n' roll music in Britain and the United States during the 1950s, this was recorded for the most part on 45rpm records; it was only after a young singer or group had notched up a significant number of successes in the sale of 'singles', that record companies would envisage a further development in their career, and often, as in the case of Elvis Presley, this development meant their moving into films rather than LPs. During the course of the Sixties, however, the number of LPs released gradually began to equal, and, in 1969, to outnumber, the quantity of 'singles' released in this country.[10]

It was the Beatles who were quickly established as trendsetters in the field of album cover design; witness, for example, the striking contrast between the cover of *Please Please Me*, 1963, with its muddled multicoloured typography, and the sophistication of the strongly side-lit black and white cover photo of *With the Beatles,* 1963, by fashion photographer Robert Freeman, which was allowed to

with the beatles

stereo

PARLOPHONE

107 The starkly lit, sophisticated photograph used on the cover of the Beatles' second LP, released in 1963, contrasted vividly with the rather clumsy cover for *Please Please Me*, released earlier the same year. The photograph was taken by Robert Freeman.

108 The ecclecticism and revivalism of much Pop design was well illustrated by the products of Dodo Designs Ltd. Their imagery ranged from Victorian fob-watches to fibreglass heads with Victorian and Edwardian hairstyles, from 1930s Hollywood stars on tea-towels and cushions to a plethora of old advertising material, including the large metal 'suns' based on emblems of 18th and 19th century insurance companies.

stand on its own without any typographic overlay. Presumably EMI were quickly persuaded of the importance of LP covers in the promotion of a particular image of the Beatles. The attention paid to the Beatles' covers was also evidence of the increasing status of pop music within a recording industry previously inclined to give precedence to classical music and film soundtracks.

With the Beatles was followed, in 1964, by *A Hard Day's Night*, the cover for which referred specifically to Pop Art in the form of Andy Warhol's serial portraiture. The Beatles' involvement with Pop Art grew primarily through Robert Fraser, the fine art dealer. It was through his mediation that the front cover and cardboard 'cut out' inserts for *Sergeant Pepper* were designed by Peter Blake and Jan Haworth. In the following year, Richard Hamilton was approached to design a cover for the Beatles' next production, a double album. Hamilton obviously felt that, given the way in which record cover design had developed by 1968, the best way to make a cover stand out from the crowd was to have nothing on it all. The *White Album* cover thus bears only the embossed words 'The BEATLES', plus

109   During the Fifties Penguin books were recognisable for their avoidance of pictorial covers. The standard format allowed only the occasional line drawing to decorate the covers of certain titles. The 1956 *Penguin Story* records that although 'in America the lurid cover is considered essential for securing mass sales of paper-backed books' Penguin had decided 'as a matter of taste to reject the American kind of cover'.

110   At the start of the Sixties, with new personnel including Germano Facetti as Art Director and Tony Godwin as Fiction Editor, a positive attempt was made to re-assert a corporate image for Penguin Books, using this grid designed by Romek Marber in 1961 for the 'Crime' series. The grid was soon used on most series of Penguin books, each being identified by a different colour, in this case orange for general fiction.

111 Subtle variations were possible with the Marber grid, such as these covers for the *Modern Poets* series.

112 Alan Aldridge's work had a dramatic impact on Penguin's previously careful, conservative cover design, introducing humour, sex, fantasy, and 'pop' styling. The revolution was short-lived; Allan Lane decided in 1967 'I'm having no more vulgar covers' and, referring to experiments in supermarket selling, 'there'll be no more gimmicky selling outside proper bookshops. Some of these frightful young marketing whizz-kids just wouldn't realize a book is not a *tin* of beans.'

a stamped consecutive numbering on the back which referred, tongue in cheek, to the edition numbering of fine art prints. Hamilton also produced a collage from material the Beatles supplied to him, a reproduction of which was included inside each cover.

The lurid colouring of the type of design from which Hamilton's *White Album* cover was intended to stand out was part of a much wider fascination with imagery associated with the effects of hallucinogenic drugs. Such imagery, and the distinctive graphic style associated with it, reached Britain during the course of 1966. A major exponent was Michael English, known earlier as the designer of objects such as the Union Jack sunglasses sold at Gear in Carnaby Street. At the end of 1966 English met Nigel Waymouth, who commissioned him to decorate his, Waymouth's, King's Road boutique, Granny takes a trip (English covered it with the giant face of an American Indian). Together, Waymouth and English worked under the studio name of Hapshash and the Coloured Coat, producing some of the most impressive of a whole crop of 'psychedelic' posters advertising records and pop concerts.

Oddly enough, in view of their 'respectable' image at the time, one of the earliest appearances on an LP cover of imagery associated with hallucinogenic drugs was produced for the Beatles LP, *Rubber Soul*, released in 1966. Here the photographic distortion of the portrait heads was coupled with the bulbous, distorted lettering which was to be used in so much 'pop' graphic work during the following years.

Work such as Martin Sharp's design for the cover of *Disraeli Gears* was part of a brief renewal of emphasis on the use of illustration rather than photography during the mid- to late-Sixties, noticeable in many forms of graphic design. When photography began to make something of a comeback on album covers towards the end of the decade it was often accompanied by distortion of either image or colour, as in Frank Zappa's *Hot Rats*. In this way, though in a different form, references to drug culture which had been embodied in much earlier illustrative work were maintained. The Sixties also saw some of the most extravagant LP covers: the production of the 3D image on the Stones' *Their Satanic Majesties Request* reputedly made it the most expensive sleeve ever produced, whilst the circular cover for the Small Faces' *Ogden's Nut Gone Flake* may have won design prizes, but the separate parts were linked by hinges so tiny that they easily ripped, whilst its shape meant that it was virtually impossible to stop the record from rolling off shelves.

Notes

1. Quoted in Georgina Howell, *In Vogue*, London 1975, pp 257-8
2. Quoted in Elizabeth Ewing, *History of 20th Century Fashion*, 2nd ed. London 1975, p 183
3. Barbara Hulanicki, *From A to Biba*, London 1983, pp 79, 82
4. Ibid., p 79
5. Mary Quant, *Quant by Quant*, London 1966, p 153
6. Ibid, p 151
7. *John French: Fashion Photographer*, Victoria and Albert Museum, London, 1985, pp 40-42
8. Barbara Hulanicki, op cit, p 98
9. *Vogue* magazine, vol.124, no.15, November 1967, p 102
10. C Booker, T Palmer, R McGough eds, *The Sixties*, Socio Pack Publications, c.1970, pages unnumbered; section on 'Pop Music'.

113 Robin Farrow and his wife,
founders of Dodo Designs Ltd., with a
selection of their goods sold in
Carnaby Street and in the antique
market in Portobello Road which
began operating in 1966. The use of
Union Jacks to decorate all kinds of
objects, as well as, the wearing of
brightly coloured military style jackets
was presumably begun in a vein of
irony and was finally overtaken by the
legitimate 'I'm backing Britain'
campaign of 1968.

114 The front cover of Oz magazine,
February 1967.

115 A selection of posters available
in Britain during 1968/9, with 'hippies'
posed in the foreground.

VARD Courier

LUXURIES BECOME NECESSITIES

When Harold Macmillan made his famous comment that 'the luxuries of the rich have become the necessities of the poor' it took the wit of the cartoonist, Trog, to point out the absurdity of the remark.[1] His cartoon showed Macmillan conducting a cabinet meeting, his ministers' chairs filled by washing machines, refrigerators, cars and the rest of the 'necessities' of the new consumer society. The fact that 85 percent of homes in 1963 had a television and 94 percent a radio was regarded as a more potent vote catcher than the faceless men of Macmillan's cabinet. As an indicator of wealth and well-being, however, the possession of consumer goods was a political trick that could only work once; as spiralling expectations outstripped actual performance, the Conservative Party slipped from popularity. In political terms, the increasingly apparent contradiction between 'private affluence, public squalor', as the economist Galbraith put it, was utterly damaging.

One of the most disturbing factors about the consumer goods/affluence indice is that it measures numbers not quality, and reflects the adman's success not the consumer's needs. That the promise of an easier or a more fulfilling life was so successful in marketing terms is shown by the numbers of people who were prepared to furnish their home through a hire purchase company. Hire purchase terms were very strict.[2] The system was based on a legal fiction: the shop or company supposedly hired the goods to the purchaser at a fixed rental for a fixed period, after which time the customer had the option of buying the goods for a nominal sum, ie £1. Hire purchase was actually a form of credit, and a costly one at that. Thus, not only did many people not own their own homes but technically neither did they own any of the shining new appliances with which they were furnished. Throughout the Sixties, as the various financial crises developed, hire purchase controls were introduced as a measure to depress an over-inflated economy. The line between confidence and investment, and hyperbole and speculation was a narrow one; the problem of living beyond one's means ('On the HP') was something that applied to individuals, as well as to the state.

116, 117 The 'Courier' shaver was designed by Kenneth Grange in 1963. The company's advertising, and the name of the product, focused attention on the shaver's portability. Purchasers were urged to keep it in the glove compartment of their car and 'shave when you want and where you want'. The marketing strategy was not able to secure enough sales, in spite of its award-winning design and superb engineering.

143

118 Hoover's 'Keymatic' washing machine is an example of the increasing automation of large household appliances during the Sixties. The machine was supplied with a 'keyplate' which allowed the user to select one of four different programmes, which the machine would then complete on its own.

TECHNOLOGY IN THE HOME

One of the most often quoted applications of technology developed for the space programme was the non-stick frying pan, and in many ways this is a typical example of the way in which the domestic appliance industry benefited from developments in other fields, rather than precipitating them themselves. This was certainly the case with the exciting developments made in the post-war period with synthetic materials. By the Sixties new materials had radically altered many of the assumptions at the core of the design process, and changed the basic vocabulary of 'modern' goods. In particular, the possibilities opened up by moulded plastics and lightweight nylons coupled with the miniaturisation made possible by the development of the transistor, completely altered the traditional relationship between casing and workings, and between size and weight. Portable versions of televisions, radios and record players were all developed, and in forms which no longer plagiarised furniture. Appliances like washing machines and cookers, however, were still based on mechanical engineering, which had not radically altered since the beginning of the century, but if they could not be miniaturised they could at least be increasingly automated.

In spite of the input of new technology into the appliance industry, there is the suspicion that modernity was only skin deep in many cases. Every year saw a crop of 'new models'. What in fact was new, in many examples, was not an improvement in efficiency or performance, but an alteration in the design of the casing; a type of design obsolescence. At the same time there is a good argument that, with notable exceptions such as companies like Kenwood,

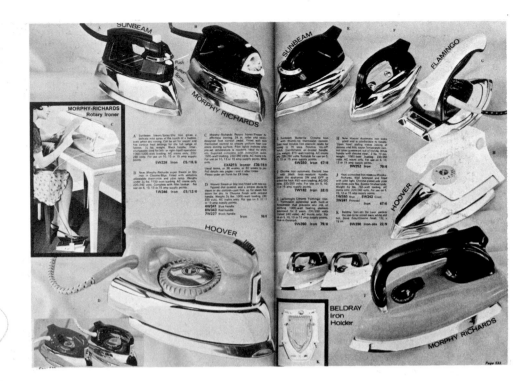

119 A selection of irons, available by mail order from Grattan, Summer 1966. Typically almost all of these models had seen no new design input since the Fifties.

120 The Kenwood 'Chef', the body of which was designed in 1960 by Kenneth Grange. The shape became so well accepted that, although Kenwood updated the mixer's mechanics suring the Seventies, they decided to keep the form of the body virtually unchanged.

121 The Morphy Richards 'TOS' toaster was introduced in 1961 and sold for £5 10s. Both the internal mechanism and the exterior casing were significant improvements on the previous model produced in the mid-Fifties. The Sixties model had the look of a precision instrument, with a clean outline, a polished chromium cover and Bakelite ends.

Hotpoint and Morphy Richards, manufacturers did not even employ this minimum of design input; they were content to repeat the same stylistic cliches left over from the Fifties. The *Which?* report on 19 inch black and white television sets in 1966 illustrated 20 leading models, ranging in price from £68 to £79, presenting a depressing picture of dull conformity.[3] It was only with the introduction of the Rank Bush Murphy coloured television in 1967, that an element of exciting design and choice was introduced into an industry that was supposed to be a symbol of modern life.

Televisions are a particularly interesting case study, because they exemplify the way in which the manufacturers of consumer goods showed little concern for the consumers themselves. The most obvious example of this was the pitiful quality of after-purchase servicing. Guarantees were virtually non-existent, or meaningless, as they excluded labour charges and carriage. For the consumer the other problem with televisions was the speed with which they became obsolescent, through technological 'advances'. With the introduction of BBC2 in 1964, televisions had to be fitted with dual standard controls, so that they could receive both 405 lines and 625 lines. The introduction of colour in 1967 was bound to make the old black and white sets redundant. With quality improving and prices dropping in relative terms, those who waited or rented stood to gain the most.

122 Introduced in 1967, the Rank Bush Murphy television set, produced in four colours, had a plastic rather than a wood casing and was a belated attempt to find a form appropriate to the technological advances made in the field of telecommunications.

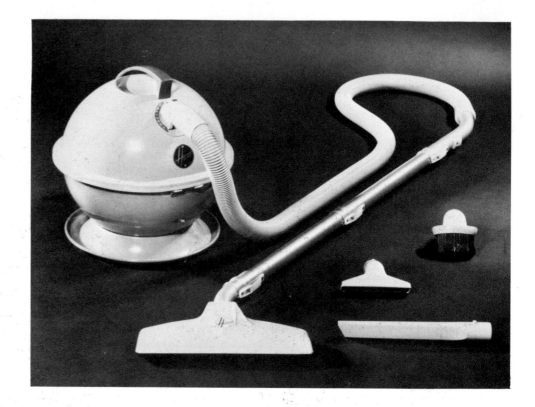

123 During the Fifties and Sixties designers often suggested the efficiency of electrical goods through smooth, clean lines, or reference to space travel. The appearance and name of Hoover's 'Constellation' vacuum cleaner implied that the application of sophisticated space-age technology would guarantee the appliance's more than adequate performance of such mundane tasks as sweeping floors.

LESS WORK MORE PLAY?

One of the major factors influencing the appearance of electrical goods was the need to sell them to women, in particular to 'housewives' – married women in the home. Traditionally designers had increased the quantity of surface decoration on such goods since it was widely believed that this appealed to women. By the Sixties the idea that goods were 'labour saving' had, through the efforts of designers and advertisers, come to be associated with smooth, clean outlines, and with pared down shapes which were easily cleaned. So persuasive was the myth of 'labour saving' devices that it was commonly assumed that women were 'freed' to pursue careers or reap the benefits of newly acquired free time, (a Hotpoint washing machine was actually called the 'Liberator'). In fact, as recent studies have shown, the average number of hours spent by housewives on housework did not significantly alter for those women who did not go out to work. [4] Increased automation and the improvement in living conditions in the post-war period removed much of the sheer drudgery from housework. But, the higher standards of cleanliness, tidiness and efficiency which housewives were encouraged to meet by the *really* bright', 'Whiter than White' messages of advertisers, meant that the time saved by so-called 'labour saving' devices was displaced into a self-perpetuating search for the unattainable.

For the increasingly large numbers of women in part or full-time work, the age of consumer goods was something of a mixed blessing. Many women gave as their reason for working the need to find the money to buy the very consumer

124, 125 An American advertising executive was quoted by Vance Packard as saying that 'if you tell the housewife that by using your washing machine, drier or dishwasher she can be left free to play bridge, you're dead!... Instead you should emphasize that the appliances free her to have more time with her children and to be a better mother.'

goods that were supposed to 'liberate' them. Housework is not a job in the sense that it is a series of clearly defined tasks: cleanliness or tidiness are not objectively measurable. Indeed they are entirely relative. In practice, the actual number of hours spent on work in the home depends on the individual woman's perception of what constitutes a 'good home'. The fact is that the washing-machine can either be a powerful symbol of subjection or a symbol of liberation, depending on the attitude of the user.

Related to the idea of labour-saving domestic appliances was a tendency in advertisements to present these goods as performing functions previously carried out by domestic servants. Kenwood's slogan was 'Kenwood — your servant, Madam', while Russell Hobbs' 'Thrift' coffee pot was described as a 'tireless servant ... ready to serve perfect coffee to your personal taste at any hour'. Underlying this marketing technique was an appeal to snobbery but one which had been significantly updated to take in the Sixties notion of 'classlessness'. Now, it seemed, everyone could have a servant, since these electrical goods were available to all, regardless of their social background.

126 A photograph of the 'Standard' telephone range taken in 1963. STD (Subscriber Trunk Dialling) had only been introduced in 1959, and the Sixties saw a concerted effort to update the telephone network.

THE STAMP OF EXCELLENCE

The charge that the domestic appliance, consumer goods industry was on the whole conservative and uninterested in research or design is at variance with a dominant myth of the Sixties: the image of a modern technological state forging ahead into a bright future. Against the background of the space race, it was important for Britain to be seen to be keeping up with the progressive dream, and enormous sums of money were put into prestige projects which bore no relation to any realistic commercial return. Concorde was the most conspicuously wasteful of these, its cost spiralling from £180 million to £1,000 million during the course of the decade.

The theme of technology as a visible expression of national achievement is of course related to the need to increase exports. Two out of the four postage stamps in the 1966 British Technology issue were of the prestige sort: Jodrell Bank radio telescope and Windscale nuclear reactor, whilst the other two, the SRN6 hovercraft and British cars, were expected to do their bit for the export drive. The British cars stamp is particularly interesting as it shows in profile the E-type Jaguar sports car and the Mini; an unused variant also included the Moulton bicycle. How, or why, these three manufactured goods in particular seemed to have caught the public imagination and had come to symbolise technolgical

127 The way in which a car designed in the late Fifties came to epitomise the swinging, modern, youthful Sixties is a story in itself. The Mini was the ideal car for fast city living; it was quick off the mark at traffic lights and easy to park in small spaces and, furthermore, its deceptively large interior took five people without too much of a squeeze.

128 The Mini also included enough engineering and technical innovations for it to function as a symbol of British technological excellence. The rubber suspension system developed by Alex Molton and the way in which Alec Issigoni designed the engine to be mounted transversely across the car body in order to save space were as important as the styling of the car in its success as a symbol of modernity.

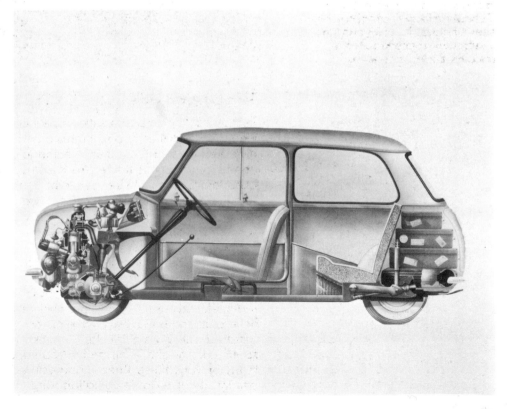

excellence and fashionable modernity at the same time, is not entirely clear. Alex Issigonis, the designer of the Mini claimed that 'it is not my job to design fashion accessories or status symbols', but that is not quite the point. [5] Something more complex is at work when a nation decides to display a car, already eight years old, painted with a Union Jack, as the centrepoint of its display at the Expo '67 show.

Traditionally, the Council of Industrial Design had promoted the canons of good taste as the way to appeal to international taste, but as John Heyes said in an article for *Design* magazine, 'Design for Export', [6] it was 'the new image of Britain created by more ephemeral design' which had 'contributed to the healthy reappraisal of Britain that is now going on throughout the world markets'. Union Jack trays triumphed where Council of Industrial Design recommended goods had previously failed to compete with Scandinavian and Italian products in the international markets.

Notes

1. Bernard Levin, *The Pendulum Years. Britain in the Sixties*, London 1970, p 212
2. Anon, 'Supplement on Borrowing', *Which?*, April 1965, p 176
3. *Which?* magazine, July 1966, p 244
4. See Ann Oakley, *Housework*, Harmondsworth, 1977
5. David Wainwright, 'Design for International Markets', *Design*, no 234, p 46
6. *Design*, no 234, pp 26-9

EPILOGUE

CENTRE POINT/ THE POST OFFICE TOWER

In 1967 a group calling itself Agitprop gathered outside Centre Point in London. Developer Harry Hyams' known reluctance to let the building, in order to allow rents and thus the building's value to increase, had made Centre Point the most conspicuous symbol of the development boom which had made millions for a few and razed whole areas of the inner cities. It was hard not to agree with the banners which claimed that 'this building is a public scandal, while thousands of people in this country are homeless or live in slum conditions'.[1] Centre Point was an important building in another way. Many argued that creative and elegant buildings like Centre Point were not the problem; it was the run of the mill slabs of concrete and steel which collectively swamped the historical character of the city. *Building Magazine*'s summary may now strike us as absurdly extravagant, but it does show how a building could embody two quite opposite meanings: 'Like the Beatles and Mary Quant ... it belongs to the decade in which English youth finally asserted itself in supreme confidence above the mediocrity of the muddle through middle of the road mentality ... Centre Point made London swing'.[2] 'London's first pop art skyscraper', as Erno Goldfinger called it.

Two years earlier the Prime Minister, Harold Wilson, and Anthony Wedgwood-Benn, the Postmaster General, opened another conspicuous addition to the London skyline. The Post Office radio tower, at 580 feet, was 200 feet higher than Centre Point, and brought a similar elegance and sleek modernity to what might have been little more than a stark concrete pillar. The presence of the Prime Minister at the opening and the media coverage which the building received, underlined the symbolic importance of this building too. The bold conception of the tower and its modern technological function exactly fitted in with the prevailing ideology of the emergence of a modern technological society. Like Centre Point, the Post Office Tower had its architectural admirers: the *Architectural Review* claimed it had 'to a quite extraordinary degree given back to the London skyline the self-respect which it had virtually surrendered before the ziggurats of Mammon'. The tower looked just as good from a distance, juxtaposed with some of London's most famous landmarks, as it did looming high over its rather unprepossessing surroundings. The role of the tower as the

129 The Post Office Tower, opened in 1965, was part of a conscious attempt by the Post Office to update its image. The sleek elegant tower soon became a powerful symbol of technological progress.

130 'Let our stamps be second to none' demanded *Design* magazine in 1960, 'for these small messengers contribute greatly to our international image.' This design by Ann and David Gillespie attempts to reconcile the horizontal format with the long thin shape of the Post Office Tower.

acceptable face of modern architecture was confirmed by the issue of two postage stamps in 1965 to commemorate its opening.

The way in which two architecturally outstanding buildings acquired diametrically opposite meanings is symbolic of a decade which provides so many contradictory impressions. From the standpoint of the Eighties, the decade offers ammunition for both sides of the political fence. David Edgar, the playwright, writing on the recent Band Aid concert saw the revival of youthful idealism, reminiscent of the late Sixties, as a challenge to the Left to rediscover the idealism it had generated in the late Sixties.[4] In contrast, Norman Tebbit, repeating standard Tory doctrine, sees our current malaise as stemming from 'the era and attitudes of post-war funk which gave birth to the "permissive society".' It seems we must distinguish carefully between two sorts of myths regarding the Sixties: between those such as 'Swinging London' and the 'modern technological society' which were deployed in the period itself and which obscured the actual situation, and those which have emerged since and thus belong to our current obsessions and needs.

It is perhaps proper to consider architecture at this point, because it alone has consistently survived to the present day. With time, the Post Office Tower has become British Telecom Tower and lost some of its power as a symbol of technological progress, whilst Centre Point, as the Confederation of British Industry headquarters, is no longer the focus of housing debates. But the mass of the built environment of the Sixties continues to exert a real influence. In some cases time has brought acceptance through familiarity and frequent usage, in others the sense of alienation and oppression has grown more powerful. In comparison the consumer goods of the period have proved to be as expendable as the manufacturers intended. They survive as historical leftovers, waiting to be updated by people who would love to be able to afford to replace what was once modern. Too recent to be historical, they feature in few museums' collecting policies. In an ironical inversion of traditional processes it is the most ephemeral products of the Sixties, the records, magazines, clothes and photographs which are most cherished and most often brought forward to characterise the decade. It is not surprising that ephemeral articles should remain the focus of fond memories; what is strange is that sophisticated historians of other periods should feel able to sum up the Sixties on the basis of how and when they first heard the Beatles or Bob Dylan.

A history constructed from goods traditionally found at the bottom of the hierarchy of design and the arts is in many ways consumer history. The objects in this exhibition each have a recoverable historical context, but at the same time every cry of 'I remember that' also reflects the consumer's ultimate right, in the 'consumer society', to attach meanings to any given object. The meanings of design when the focus of attention is solely on the designer are discrete and fixed, but when the consumer enters the equation, meanings are multiplied. The pattern of a design shift from imposed objective standards to a new pluralism is evident in all spheres of design in the decade, and to miss out the consumer's share would be to perpetuate a grave historical injustice. Likewise there is no such objective thing as The Sixties: it is the media and politicians who propose the existence of one Sixties, the Sixties that suit their own preoccupations.

Throughout this exhibition, we have been at pains to warn of the dangers inherent in the Sixties' capacity to generate myths. Nevertheless, one must be careful not to lose sight of the very real social achievements and gains made in the decade. At a time of increasing political reaction, we need more than ever to acknowledge what was best about the Sixties, lest it is swept away by the new Right ready to manipulate the latent emotional power of the decade. For almost a generation we have all been reaping the enormous benefits of the endeavours of what was, in the early Sixties, a small minority, and which grew to become a powerful force for betterment. The Sixties sowed the seeds of the feminist and environmentalist movements, as well as ushering in a new tolerance which culminated in liberal legislation on issues such as divorce, homosexuality, abortion and censorship. It is arguably these real achievements, rather than the shallow types of freedom commonly seen to be symbolised by objects such as the mini-skirt, and by the public lives of celebrities such as David Bailey, which are the most important legacy of the period 1960-1969.

Notes

1. Francis Wheen, *The Sixties*, London 1982
2. Anon, 'Centre Point, Symbol of the Sixties', *Building*, 24 May, 1969, p 104
3. Anon, 'Radio Campanile', *Architectural Review*. 1966, pp 123-6
4. See David Edgar, 'It wasn't so naff in the '60s after all', *The Guardian*, 7 July, 1986

BIBLIOGRAPHY

BAILEY, David (with notes by Francis Wyndham) *A Box of Pin-Ups*. London, 1965

BANHAM, Reyner (ed. Penny Sparke). *Design by Choice*. London, 1981

BAYNES, Ken. *Industrial Design and the Community*. London, 1967

BENNETT-ENGLAND, Rodney. *Dress Optional: the Revolution in Menswear*. London, 1967

BERNARD, Barbara. *Fashion in the 60s*. London, 1978

BOOKER, C., Palmer, T., McGough, R. (eds). *The Sixties*. Socio-Pack Publications Ltd, c. 1970

BOOKER, Christopher. *The Neophiliacs*. London, 1969

BUCHANAN, Colin. *Traffic in Towns: a study of the long-term problems of traffic in urban areas* (Report of the group set up by the Ministry of Transport). London, 1963

CAPLAN, David (ed). *Designers in Britain 6: a Review of Graphic and Industrial Design compiled by the Society of Industrial Artists and Designers*. London, 1964

COHN, Nik. *Today There Are No Gentlemen*. London, 1971

COLEMAN, Alice. *Utopia on Trial: Vision and Reality in Planned Housing*. London, 1985

CONSUMERS ASSOCIATION. *Which?*. 1958-

CORLEY, T. A. B. *Domestic Electrical Appliances*. London, 1966

COULSON, A. J. *Bibliography of Design in Britain 1851-1970*. London, 1979

DAILY MAIL. *Book of Furnishing, Decorating and Kitchen Plans*. London, 1966

ESHER, Lionel. *The Rebuilding of England 1940-80*. London, 1981

EWING, Elizabeth. *History of 20th Century Fashion*. 2nd ed. London, 1975

FORTY, Adrian. *Objects of Desire: Design and Society 1750-1980*. London, 1986

FAULKNER, Wendy and Arnold, Erik (eds). *Smothered by Invention*. London, 1985

GARLAND, Ken. *Ken Garland and Associates: Designers. Twenty Years' Work and Play 1962-82*. London, 1982

GARNER, Philippe. *Twentieth-Century Furniture*. Oxford, 1980

GOSLING, David and Maitland, Barry. *Design and Planning of Detail Systems*. London, 1976

GRATTAN Mail Order Catalogues, Summer/Winter, 1966-7

GREATER LONDON COUNCIL, Department of Architecture and Civic Design. *Home Sweet Home. Housing designed by the LCC and the GLC Architects 1888-1975*. London, 1976

HEBDIGE, Dick. 'Towards a Cartography of Taste 1935-1962' in *Popular Culture: Past and Present*, ed. B. Waites, T. Bennett, G. Martin. London, 1982

HEBDIGE, Dick. *Subculture and the Meaning of Style*. London, 1979

HMSO, Central Housing Advisory Committee, chaired by Sir Parker Morris. *Homes for Today and Tomorrow*. London, 1961

HOLLIDAY, J. (ed). *City Centre Redevelopment*. London, 1973

HOWELL, Georgina. *In Vogue: Six Decades of Fashion*. London, 1975

HULANICKI, Barbara. *From A to Biba*. London, 1983

INGLIS, Fred. *The Imagery of Power: the Genetics of Advertising*. London, 1972

LEVIN, Bernard. *The Pendulum Years: Britain in the Sixties*. London, 1970

LITTLEWOODS Mail Order Catalogue. Autumn/Winter 1966-7

LITTLEWOODS. *Mail Order in Britain*, 1972

LYALL, Sutherland. *The State of British Architecture*. London, 1980

LYALL, Sutherland. *Hille: 75 Years of British Furniture*. London, 1981

MACCARTHY, Fiona. *All Things Bright and Beautiful: Design in Britain 1830 to Today*. London, 1972

MACCARTHY, Fiona. *British Design Since 1880: A Visual History*. London, 1982

MACEWEN, Malcolm. *Crisis in Architecture*. London, 1974

MANCHESTER, City Planning Department. *City Centre Map*. 1967

MARRIOTT, Oliver. *The Property Boom*. London, 1967

MARWICK, Arthur. *British Society since 1945*. (Pelican Social History of Britain), Harmondsworth, 1982

MCROBBIE, Angela. 'Jackie: an Ideology of Adolescent Femininity' in *Popular Culture: Past and Present* ed. B. Waites, T. Bennett, G. Martin. London, 1982

MILLAR, J. S. *Manchester City Centre Map*. 1967

MINISTRY OF TECHNOLOGY. *Houses and People*. London, 1966

NUTTALL, Jeff. *Bomb Culture*. London, 1968

OAKLEY, Ann. *Housework*. Harmondsworth, 1977

OLINS, Wally. *The Corporate Personality: an inquiry into the nature of corporate identity*. London (Design Council), 1978

OLINS, Wally. 'The Industrial Designer in England', forthcoming article in *Did Britain Make It?* London (Design Council), 1986

PAPANEK, Victor. *Design for the Real World*. New York, 1971

PHILLIPS, Barty. *Conran and the Habitat Story*. London, 1984

RODGERS, Brian. 'Manchester: metropolitan planning by collaboration and consent; or civic hope frustrated' in *Regional Cities in the U.K. 1890-1980*. London, 1986

RUSSELL, Gordon. *Looking at Furniture*. London, 1984

SALVATION ARMY. *For God's Sake Care*. London, 1968

SPARKE, Penny. *An Introduction to Design and Culture in the Twentieth Century*. London, 1986

SPARKE, Penny. *Furniture*. London, 1986

SUDJIC, Deyan. *Cult Objects*. London, 1985

TAYLOR, Nicholas. *The Village in the City*. London, 1973

THORGERSON, Storm and Dean, Roger. *The Album Cover Album*. Surrey, 1977

WHEEN, Francis. *The Sixties*. London, 1982

WHITE, H. R. *The Continuing Conurbation. Change and Development in Greater Manchester*. Farnborough, Hants, 1980

WOODHAM, Jonathan. *The Industrial Designer and the Public*. London, 1983

Articles

Anon. 'At Home With Entertainment', *Ideal Home,* September 1966, pp 83-9

Anon. 'Times Supplement on Industrialized Building', *The Times,* 21 March 1966

Anon. 'Radio Campanile', *Architectural Review,* 1966, p 123

Anon. 'Centre Point. Symbol of the Sixties', *Building,* 24 May 1968, pp 99-106

BAYNES, Ken and Kate. 'Behind the Scene', *Design,* 212, 1966, pp 20-9

BEAZLEY, Elizabeth. 'Supermarkets', *Architectural Review,* 1967, pp 329-34

CARR, Richard. 'The "For God's Sake" Campaign', *Design,* 236, 1968, pp 32-6

CORNFORD, Christopher. 'Cold Rice Pudding and Revisionism', *Design,* 231, 1968, pp 46-8

FLEETWOOD, Michael. 'Building revisited: Alton Estate, Roehampton', *The Architects' Journal,* March 1977, pp 593-603

HARRIS, Michael. 'The Runcorn Busway', *Modern Transport,* 1978, pp 186-90

HEYES, John. 'Design for Export', *Design,* 234, 1968, pp 26-9

HUGHES-STANTON, Corin. 'What Comes After Carnaby Street?', *Design,* 230, 1968, pp 42-3

JENKINS, Eddie. 'Project Revisited: Halton Brow, Runcorn', *The Architects' Journal,* 21 March 1979, pp 585-96

JONES, D. A. N. 'Keep Swinging', *The New Statesman,* 17 April 1984

MCNAB, Archie. 'Shop Shape', *Design,* 163, 1962, pp 28-31

MILLAR, J. S. 'Planning in Manchester – a time of rapid change', *Town Planning Institute Journal,* April 1968, pp 49-53

PEVSNER, Nikolaus. 'Alton Estate', *Architectural Review,* July 1959, pp 1-16

POND, Edward. 'Design This Way', *Painting and Decorating.* October 1968, pp 18-21

RAYNER, Claire. 'Super Detail for Supermarket Shopping', *Design,* 240, 1968, pp 60-2

REILLY, Paul. 'The Challenge of Pop', *Architectural Review,* October 1967, pp 255-7

SMITH, Peter. 'Runcorn main Shopping Centre', *The Architects' Journal,* 21 June 1972

SWENARTON, Mark. 'Should we stop Exhibiting Design?', *London Journal,* vol. 6, no.1, 1980, pp 112-115

TAYLOR, Nicholas. 'The Failure of Housing', *Architectural Review,* November 1967

VARLEY, Peter. 'The Toymakers of Britain', *Design,* 227, 1967, pp 23-9

WAINWRIGHT, David. 'Design for International Markets', *Design,* 234, 1968, pp 40-6

Thesis

SENEVIRATNE, Denise. *'Swinging London': the construction of an image,* unpublished dissertation, Manchester Polytechnic, 1985

Exhibition Catalogues

Arts Council, *David Bailey: Black and White Memories,* 1985

Liverpool, Walker Art Gallery. *The Art of the Beatles,* 1984

London, The Boilerhouse Project. *Kenneth Grange at the Boilerhouse: an exhibition of British Product Design,* 1983

London, The Boilerhouse Project, *Images for Sale: 21 Years of Graphics, Advertising, Packaging and Commercials from Design and Art Direction,* ed. Stephen Bayley, 1983

London, Museum of London. *Mary Quant's London,* 1973-4

London, Royal Festival Hall. *Fifty Penguin Years,* 1985

London, Victoria and Albert Museum. *The Way We Live Now: Design for interiors 1950 to the Present Day,* 1979

London, Victoria and Albert Museum. *John French: Fashion Photographer,* 1985

London, Whitechapel Art Gallery. *Modern Chairs 1918-1970,* 1970

Manchester Polytechnic. *Design Process: Inside Story of Familiar Products 1984*

Philadelphia, Museum of Art. *Design Since 1945,* 1983